Life is Hard, but...

God is GOOD!

By David Brown

For Reorders Contact:
Walk on the Water Faith Church
PO Box 1124
Osage Beach, Mo. 65065-1124 USA
573-348-9777 / Web: www.faithman.org

Life is Hard, but...God is Good!
Copyright © 1997 by David Brown
P. O. Box 32121
Amarillo, TX 79120
ISBN 0-9659263-0-3

Cover Design and book production by:
DB & Associates Design & Distribution
P.O. Box 52756, Tulsa, OK 74152
Cover Illustration is protected by the 1976 United States Copyright Act.
Copyright © 1997 by DB & Associates Design Group, Inc.

CONTENTS

DEDICATION

    This book is lovingly dedicated to my wonderful wife and best friend, Connie, an able minister of the New Testament, one who has bravely gone through the hard times, one who has "put up" with me, and the greatest encourager of my life! Thank you sweetie! I love you!

David

FOREWORD

"As soon as we realize that LIFE IS HARD, we will be more thankful for the blessings we receive in this life, and a whole lot happier!"

Something exploded in me when I heard these words spoken by my long time friend, evangelist James Maloney. Life is hard! It really is! Life gets so tough for some people, they choose a suicidal death over an agonizing life. Others choose slower forms of self destruction, such as drugs, alcohol, and illicit sex. Why? Because life is hard!

Some destroy their mental, emotional, social, and marital lives through more subtle means such as selfishness, withdrawal, or workaholism. Why? Because it seems that there is just no such thing as life working out automatically.

There is no fantasy land of pure joy, gladness, and pleasure. There is no gain without pain. There is no glory without the guts to face obstacles, roadblocks, hardships, and negative circumstances.

Programmed by movies with happy endings, light hearted television sitcoms, positive thinking seminars, panacea promising politicians, and best seller paperback fictions, we want to believe that someday we will be able to exclaim, "It's a wonderful life!" Of course we desire to attain this wonderful life without a great deal of effort, heartache, or headache of our own.

Our society is addicted to addiction itself. Escapism has become our lifestyle, whether it manifests in drug abuse, over eating, pleasure seeking, or even religion. Life is hard! We can deny it, try to forget it, or even create new philosophies and theologies in an effort to supersede it, but it will all be to no avail. Sooner or later reality will set in again, maybe through the death of a loved one, or the loss of a job, a divorce, or maybe by the personal rejection of a longtime friend. It is a lesson we are constantly learning.

Life is hard! We may try to escape it, but when we sober up, come down, get alone, or lie awake at night, it taunts us, haunts us, depresses us, and oppresses us. Life is hard! Life is really, really hard!

This may all sound a little discouraging; however, I do have some good news. Perhaps I have already hit a nerve. Maybe you are hurting and you picked up this book in the hope of somehow medicating the pain. I've been there, too.

I, like you and everyone I've ever met, have suffered the pain of living, but I do have some good news for you. *Oh give thanks unto the Lord, for he is good, for his mercy endureth forever:"* *Psalms 107:1.* God is the one who can make a difference for you! In His book, The Bible, He shows us how to deal with the hardships of life through His **goodness!**

Chapter 1

GOOD NEWS AND BAD NEWS

I have some good news and some bad news for you. The good news is, "God is good." The bad news is, "life is hard." Life is hard, but God is good! This statement may sound contradictory, but it is not. "If God is so good," many ask, "why is life so hard?" The problem is, some people view every event in life as God's will; however, this is not accurate.

MANY THINGS THAT HAPPEN IN LIFE
ARE NOT THE WILL OF GOD!

We must stop assuming that every negative thing we experience in life is some sick joke played on us by a cruel creator. God's word, the Bible, identifies Satan as another spiritual entity, who is seeking to influence our lives. Jesus gives us valuable information about Satan in the Gospel of John. *"The thief cometh not, but for to steal, and to kill, and to destroy." John 10:10a.* Satan is the thief that comes to steal good things from your life. He comes to kill every trace of life within you.

Ultimately my friend, he desires to see you utterly destroyed for eternity. What am I saying? I am saying that you have an enemy and I'm not talking about your business competitor. I am talking about the devil. Satan! He is real and he is your greatest enemy, but you also have a friend.

GOD is your friend! Jesus is the Son of God, and He came to this earth to reveal to us the character, the behavior, and the very heart of God.

Listen to what Jesus said about God the Father in comparison to the Devil. *"The thief cometh not, but for to steal, and to kill, and to destroy: I AM COME THAT THEY MIGHT HAVE LIFE, AND THAT THEY MIGHT HAVE IT MORE ABUNDANTLY." John 10:10*

Satan has inspired everything in this life that can be called sin. Sin can be defined as anything that misses the mark of God's perfection. God is perfect, and He desires perfection and wholeness throughout His creation, which includes you and your life. Therefore, anything that is not perfect, is outside the will of God, and actually reveals the mark of Satan on this world and on all of our lives.

Sin has many various effects on creation. Sickness and disease are the products of sin. Poverty, famine, shame, guilt, strife, prejudice, wars, divorce, heartbreak, accidents, birth defects, and suffering in all forms can be classified as the aftermath of sin and rebellion against God. The truth is if Adam, the first man, had not sinned against God, none of us would be experiencing the hard life we are now experiencing.

Now, don't get all bent out of shape with great-grandfather, Adam. We have all sinned, but God is our friend! He loves us and He is on our side. He did something to help us! Jesus came to this earth to give us "abundant life." Does abundant life mean life will no longer be hard? No!

Abundant life means that God will pour His eternal and powerful life force through you to such an extent that it will conquer anything that Satan, sin, and suffering can throw at you.

The Bible says that through faith in God, you can be an overcomer! It also says that He will make you to be more than a conqueror through His love. Faith does not make life easy, but it does make good things in life possible! *"All things are possible to him that believeth."   Mark 9:23*

The very reason God sent His son, Jesus, into the world, was to bring His goodness into our hard and hurtful situations. The message of the Bible is called "the Gospel." "Gospel" means "GOOD NEWS." The Gospel message of the Bible, and of true Christianity is that THERE IS A GOD IN HEAVEN, AND HE WANTS TO DO GOOD THINGS FOR PEOPLE. This was the theme of Jesus' entire earthly ministry.

> *"Jesus came into Galilee, preaching the gospel of the kingdom of God, and saying, The time is fulfilled, and the kingdom of God is at hand: repent ye, and believe the gospel."*
>
> *Mark 1:14-15*

Jesus' message was the good news of the kingdom of God. The word "kingdom" is defined as "rule, realm, and royalty." Jesus taught that the time had come. God's kingdom was at hand or "within their reach."   Anytime they desired, they could reach out and take hold of God's kingdom! God's rule was now available to them. They had complicated and damaged their lives.

Perhaps it was time to let God take over! God's realm was now available. They could now enter into a spiritual relationship with God and enjoy His presence and power.

God's royalty was also available. People can now be "born again" and adopted into God's royal family.

Actually, everything God is and everything God can possibly do for a human being is included in the rule, realm, and royalty of God. I am not sure we comprehend what Jesus was actually saying.

What He said is this: GOD IS AVAILABLE TO YOU NOW! RIGHT NOW, GOD WILL TOUCH, ENTER, AND TRANSFORM YOUR LIFE! ANYTIME YOU DESIRE GOD, AND EVERYTHING HE CAN DO FOR YOU, REACH OUT FOR HIM! GOD IS AVAILABLE! YOU CAN REACH OUT AND TAKE HOLD OF GOD AND PULL HIM INTO YOUR LIFE!

Wow! It just doesn't get any better than this. This is what the Gospel is all about. Jesus bled and died to make this possible for us. He told us how to reach out and take hold of God and His kingdom.

Simply repent and believe! To repent means "to change your mind and direction." We are to change our minds about sin, about God, and about making our own decisions. You must allow God to call the shots. WE must be willing to follow Him, obey Him, and allow Jesus Christ to be the Lord (owner and controller) of our lives!

Secondly, Jesus said, we are to "Believe the Gospel." Repent and then simply believe the good news that God and everything He offers is available to you because of the price Jesus Christ paid for you on the cross. He suffered in your place, died in your name, and acted as your substitute. He took the curse, so you could be blessed.[1] He bore your sin so you could be forgiven, cleansed, and receive eternal life.[2] He carried your sickness, so that you can now be healed.[2] He suffered rejection, so that you can now be perfectly accepted with God.[3]

What Jesus bore, you no longer need to bear. What Jesus paid for as your Redeemer, you can now receive freely from Heaven, if you will only believe. Remember, *"All things are possible to him that believeth."*[4]

To live a life marked with the continual blessing of God, we must believe the Gospel of the Kingdom. We must be constantly changing our minds and direction from that which is evil and unclean, to that which is good and holy! We must live by faith. We must have faith in God that He is a good God, and that He is a rewarder of diligent seekers.[5]

His blessings will immediately begin to manifest to us. *"Unto you first God, having raised up His son Jesus, SENT HIM TO BLESS YOU, IN TURNING AWAY EVERY ONE OF YOU FROM HIS INIQUITIES," ACTS 3:26*

Do you want to receive the blessings of God? Do you want to experience His goodness? The first step is to receive Jesus Christ into your life. Reach out and pull Him into your life right now! You might want to pray something like this. . .

Dear Lord Jesus,
I need you and I need your goodness. I know now
that you are available to me. You will pour your
goodness into my life and remove all of my sin,
rebellion, and guilt by your own blood. I turn away
from my sin and accept you into my life. I know that
you are alive and I decide to follow you for the rest of
my life as you strengthen me! Fill my life with your
goodness and blessings. I trust you with my whole

*heart.   You are now my Saviour, my Lord, and my
God!   Amen!*

(I want to help you. If you will complete and mail the form found on page 128, I will send you some information that will help you!)

Wonderful! That was the first step into blessing! Let me quickly share with you eight keys to victory and blessing in life. Then we will discuss some of the HARD THINGS in life and how God can HELP you to deal with them.

First, begin to practice the following simple principles. They are all found in the Bible and they will prove to be channels of blessing into your life.

"EIGHT KEYS TO VICTORY AND BLESSING IN LIFE"

1.   TELL SOMEONE ABOUT YOUR DECISION! [6]
➡ The confession of your faith will strengthen you and help you to sense the reality of your experience with God.

2.   ATTEND CHURCH! [7]
➡ Find a strong Bible teaching, Holy Spirit filled church where the believers pray and receive answers from God.

3. TALK TO THE LORD![8]
➡ Pray. Talk openly to God like you would your best friend. Ask for His help and guidance.

4. READ THE BIBLE! [9]
➡ Start with the new testament.

5. BE BAPTIZED IN WATER! [10]
➡ This act of obedience will strengthen your faith and commitment to the Lord.

6. BE FILLED WITH THE HOLY SPIRIT! [11]
➡ A pastor or experienced Christian can help you to receive the infilling of the Spirit along with its accompanying sign, your own spiritual prayer language.

7. MAKE CHRISTIAN FRIENDS! [12]
➡ You need Godly positive relationships to keep you strong.

8. PARTICIPATE IN SMALL GROUPS![13]
➡ There are two types of small groups you need to be a part of. You will find support and friendship in "fellowship groups." (Some churches fulfill this need through Sunday school classes). You will also begin to grow and gain strength by joining a "ministry team"

where you will learn to serve through practical service, (your church will help you to become involved in serving).

**DON'T FORGET! THE GOOD NEWS IS THIS:
"GOD IS GOOD AND HE WANTS TO MAKE
YOUR LIFE BRAND NEW!"**

Chapter 2

"I'M SICK AND TIRED OF
BEING SICK AND TIRED"

or

What do you do when you're sick and can't get well?

One of the hardest things we experience in life is the suffering that is associated with sickness. Sickness has its own pain. Sometimes the pain is paralyzing and debilitating for the sufferer. The hardships of sickness are also shared with those closely associated with the sick.

What sadness fills the home that has a diseased or deformed child! What pain torments the hearts of children who witness the slow and agonizing death of elderly parents! What darkness and depression consumes the family that loses a young mother or father in the prime of their life!

I know a little bit about this subject, myself. I was six years old when my father, at only thirty years of age, suddenly passed away from a heart attack. My mother discovered, along with my brother, sister, and myself, that life really is hard. Yes, life is hard, but always remember; GOD IS GOOD! Let's talk about sickness, and the goodness of God!

Throughout human history, sickness, disease, and malady has afflicted the human race with pain. We have grown so accustomed to it, we assume that disease is normal and natural, however the truth is that God never intended for disease to be the normal ongoing human experience.

No disease ever manifested in a human body until after the first man, Adam, rebelled and sinned against God. When God created Adam and his wife Eve, He blessed them.[1] As blessed people, made in the image and likeness of God, they had no disease in their bodies.[2] Deuteronomy clearly teaches that sickness is a curse, and that health is a blessing from God. Sickness is not God's plan for our lives. The Bible reveals that health and wholeness is God's perfect will for people.

A casual reading of the history of the Jews as recorded in Exodus, Leviticus, and Deuteronomy will show that God frequently allowed disease when sin was committed. Various scriptures teach plainly however, that though God may allow disease, Satan is the true author of it. Satan is the one who tempts us with sin. He is the author of sin, and sin is the father of disease. Yes, Satan is the originator of sickness and disease. He busies himself inflicting his pain upon people.[3]

When Adam sinned, he opened a spiritual door for Satan to become the god of this world, and to begin to oppress people with sickness, disease, pain, and all sorts of other problems. Adam's own immediate family became acutely problematic by suffering the loss of their wealth, and by becoming cursed with jealousy, hatred, and murder. Now that man is under the curse of sin, disease runs rampant throughout creation.

We are stricken often with sickness, not necessarily because we have personally sinned, although this is certainly possible, but simply because we live in a world where germs, viruses, contagion, and corruption fill our environment. Certainly our sins can make us susceptible to various diseases such as cancer caused by the use of tobacco products, or HIV and other sexually transmitted diseases caused by illicit sex. However, no direct sin is necessary to bring sickness. We get sick because sickness is in our world. Sickness is in the world because sin is in the world.

God is not personally striking us with these maladies. We as a race in Adam, have stricken ourselves with our own sin. We have incurred the curse of sin and death upon ourselves. However, there is GOOD NEWS!

> *"For the law of the spirit of life in Christ Jesus hath*
> *made me free from the law of sin and death!"*
>
> *Romans 8:2*

God has done something about our sickness and disease. After all, He is a healing God!

> *"I am the Lord that healeth thee!"*   *Exodus 15:26*

God introduces Himself as the God who heals! God has never introduced Himself as "the God that inflicteth thee with disease and pain." He is a lifting, loving, saving, and healing God. He loves you! He does not make you sick. Rather, He can grant the strength, vitality, power, and grace to give you a new, robust and divine health!

Have you ever thought about the fact that everywhere Jesus went during His earthly life and ministry, He healed sick people? Why did He spend such a large amount of His time alleviating pain and suffering? We know that everything Jesus did was the will of God the Father in Heaven. *1 John 3:8* states that the purpose for the Son of God being manifested in the earth was to *"destroy the works of the devil!"* Therefore, disease is a work of the devil, for Jesus destroyed it continually. Furthermore, healing must be God's will, for Jesus made a habit of making the sick well again!

> *"How God anointed Jesus of Nazareth with the Holy Ghost and with power: who went about doing good, and healing all that were oppressed of the devil..."*
>
> *Acts 10:38*

Jesus not only healed during His earthly ministry, but continues to heal today!

> *"Jesus Christ the same yesterday and to day and forever."*
>
> *Hebrews 13:8*

When we exercise faith in God, and what He did for us through Christ's death on the cross, we can be healed of any disease!

> *"Jesus went about healing every sickness and every disease among the people."*
>
> *Matthew 9:35*

At the cross, Jesus Christ paid our price, bore our curse, and died our death. He was our substitute. We no longer need to bear what He bore for us. He bore our sin and sickness; therefore, we no longer need to bear them. We can be saved and healed.

Doesn't it make sense that if sickness is a curse of sin, then the remedy for sin will also be the remedy for sickness? Isaiah prophesied hundreds of years before Jesus was born about His death on the cross and what it would accomplish redemptively for all of mankind.

"Surely He hath BORNE our griefs, (sicknesses) and CARRIED our sorrows (pains): yet we did esteem Him stricken, smitten of God, and afflicted. But He was wounded FOR OUR transgressions, He was bruised FOR OUR iniquities: the chastisement of OUR peace was UPON HIM; and WITH HIS STRIPES WE ARE HEALED."

Isaiah 53:4-5

You see, the same blood that Jesus shed for the cleansing of sin from our spirits, also furnishes us with healing for our sick bodies! If faith in Christ's blood brings forgiveness, then faith in His blood can also bring healing!

Matthew's gospel confirms that this is an accurate application of Isaiah's prophecy, noting that Jesus fulfilled it by healing those who were physically sick.[4]

Are you sick and tired of being sick and tired? Place your trust in Jesus the Healer today! He can make you healthy and strong! Why don't you do what one woman in the Bible did?

"And a certain woman, which had an issue of blood twelve years, and had suffered many things of many physicians, and had spent all that she had, and was nothing bettered, but rather grew worse, when she had heard of Jesus, came in the press behind, and touched his garment. For she said, If I may touch but his clothes, I shall be whole. And straightway the fountain of her blood was dried up; and she felt in her body that she was healed of that plague. And Jesus, immediately knowing in himself that virtue had gone

> *out of him, turned him about in the press, and said, Who touched my clothes? And his disciples said unto him, Thou seest the multitude thronging thee, and thou sayest, Who touched me? And he looked round about to see her who had done this thing. But the woman fearing and trembling, knowing what was done in her, came and fell down before him, and told him all the truth. And he said unto her, Daughter, thy faith hath made thee whole; go in peace and be whole of thy plague."*
>
> *Mark 5:25-34.*

This woman did four specific things that enabled her to receive a healing miracle in her body!

1. *SHE HEARD ABOUT JESUS!*

Romans 10:17 states that faith comes when we hear what the Word of God says. The Word tells us about Jesus! You are hearing about the healing power of Jesus right now!

2. *SHE SOUGHT JESUS!*

She went where He could be found! You may find Him in a strong local church, or while reading your Bible. Jesus the Healer may come to you through a Christian friend, or you may find Him all by yourself in a place of private prayer!

3. *SHE TOUCHED JESUS!*

She contacted Him. She touched His clothes. And though many had touched Him with the feeling of their hands, she touched Him with the "faith of her heart!" Your point of contact with Jesus might be the anointing of oil by Church elders.[5] It could also be through the laying on of a believer's hands,[6] or simply through your own prayer of faith,[7] similar to the one you prayed for salvation.

4. *SHE TALKED ABOUT JESUS!*

She said, *"If I can just touch his clothes, I shall be whole."* Talk about Jesus! Speak your faith. Say out loud what you expect, and continue to say it until your miracle happens.[8]

Jesus said that her faith had made her whole! Of course it was His healing virtue that effected the miracle of healing and restoration in her body, but it was her faith that tapped into His healing power!

Faith reaches out and "takes a miracle from God!" Faith reaches past the ordinary and takes the extraordinary! Faith reaches beyond the natural into the supernatural realm of God! Faith is your key to miracles!

It's not up to God to decide to heal you. He already decided to heal you. It's actually up to you now, to go to God and receive your healing by faith! Your healing is already paid for by the blood of Jesus Christ!

". . .what things soever ye desire, when ye pray,
believe that ye receive them, and ye shall have them."

Mark 11:24

Do what the woman with the issue of blood did, she believed and then received! Believing always involves HEARING, SEEK-ING, TOUCHING, and TALKING! Are you sick and tired of being sick and tired? God's goodness is guaranteed when you believe and obey His Word!

GOD'S GOODNESS IS GUARANTEED WHEN YOU...

➤ "HEAR, SEEK, TOUCH AND TALK!"

Both forgiveness and healing are bought by the same divine blood. The same conditions must be met to receive forgiveness or healing. To be forgiven or healed, you must turn from your past. To be forgiven or healed, you must focus your faith on God's future for you!

HEAR about Jesus! SEEK Him with your whole heart! TOUCH Him with your faith! TALK like a believer talks expecting a miracle from God! Dig in! Take your stand!

Believe you receive your miracle! Make a quality decision to **HEAR, SEEK, TOUCH, AND TALK!**

I have seen literally thousands of people receive miraculous healings during my two decades of ministry! I've stood on the beautifully carpeted platforms of North American churches, and I've also stood on the crude wooden platforms of open air evangelistic crusades in poverty stricken third world countries.

I have found that wherever and whenever true faith in Jesus Christ is exercised, the blind see, the deaf hear, the lame walk, cancer melts away, and pain disappears! God can and will heal you, if you will only believe![9]

A single mother in her early twenties was brought to our "Fiesta de Milagros" (Party of Miracles) Campaign in Siguatepeque, Honduras. She had suffered a stroke leaving her paralyzed on one side of her body and she was in much pain. Electric shock treatments had been administered to her at the local hospital in an attempt to restore the mobility of her muscles, but it was to no avail. A friend brought her to the meeting and sat her on the back row, hoping for a miracle. I taught a simple message of "good news," entitled "Jesus Wants To Heal You."

I read and spoke directly from the Bible, sharing several recorded stories of people who had been healed by Jesus. I reminded the people that Jesus Christ is the same yesterday, today, and forever.[10] I also shared stories about people who had been healed in our meetings over the past few years.

After I finished speaking, I invited all who were sick and diseased to bow their heads and pray a simple prayer of faith with me. In the authority of Jesus' name, I commanded Satan to loose them from the shackles of sickness, then I asked God in Heaven to heal them! I then encouraged the people to activate their faith by doing something they couldn't have done before. They began to move, jump, walk around, and praise the Lord! Many hands went up in the air signifying that they had received a healing miracle from the risen Saviour, Jesus Christ! The young paralyzed mother, sadly had not experienced any change in her body up to this point. I asked for those who had been instantly healed and would be willing to share their story, to come forward to the platform. The paralyzed woman saw several people begin to walk toward the front of the crowd, and she began to think . . .

"The stories that the preacher told . . . they came from the Bible. The Bible is God's Word. The Bible is true. Those miracles really happened. The people that the preacher talked about really did get healed. If they were healed, then I can be healed! I am going to trust God to heal me too!"

Then she did a strange thing! She stood up and began to slowly walk toward the platform. Even though I had only asked for those who had been immediately healed, she began walking toward the front BY FAITH! She decided that she would be healed too, and since the healed people were walking to the front, SHE WOULD WALK TO THE FRONT! She was literally WALKING BY FAITH! By the time she reached the platform, the pain was gone! All of her paralysis had disappeared!

She was totally, 100 percent whole! Jesus had healed her. Her faith had made her whole! She had met the conditions of GOD'S GOODNESS GUARANTEE! She had HEARD, SOUGHT, TOUCHED, AND TALKED her way into a healing miracle by FAITH!

Are you sick and tired of being sick and tired? You can be healed, if you will ONLY BELIEVE! God will heal you.

Remember, GOD IS GOOD!

Chapter 3

"WHY?"

or

What do you do, when you don't know why?

Bartimaeus was a man who lived in the city of Jericho during the earthly ministry of Jesus. In the tenth chapter of Mark's gospel we are told that he sat on the road side and begged for his living, because he was blind. Sitting there in the dusty ditch, he must have constantly asked himself the ever haunting question, "Why?"

Bartimaeus' sight had been stolen from him. He was blind. Whatever he might have been, whatever he might have accomplished, however he might have succeeded in life, was now impossible. He had no Seeing Eye Dog, and there was no braille. The fact was inescapable then, just as it is today. Blind people simply cannot do everything that sighted people can do.

Not only had his physical sight been stolen, but his vision for life had been torn from him as well. Bartimaeus was a beggar, this was his lot in life. Pushed to the side of the road, and out of peoples' way, he was left with the worst of his conditions, he was BEWIL-DERED!

Why?" This is the question that he asked himself, "WHY am I blind? WHY did this terrible tragedy have to happen to me? WHY has my potential been stifled? WHY must I suffer the humiliation of being a beggar? WHY must I sit in the dirt and hold out my hand to everyone passing by? Why do most of them look the other way and hurry past me?"

This was the condition of Bartimaeus on the day Jesus passed by. Bartimaeus evidently had heard about Jesus, and he had heard that this prophet from Nazareth had performed some amazing miracles.

When Jesus touched them, the deaf heard, the lame walked, and the blind saw! When he heard that it was Jesus who was about to pass by, faith sprang up in his heart and he began to cry out, *"Jesus, son of David, have mercy on me!"*

Some of the people standing around began to discourage Bartimaeus. Mark says that they, *"Charged him that he should hold his peace."* "Shut up little blind man. Jesus doesn't have time for you!", they may have said, but Bartimaeus just got louder. *"JESUS, SON OF DAVID, HAVE MERCY ON ME!"*

Bartimaeus had asked, "Why?" long enough. This was his window of opportunity, and he had to seize it. *"JESUS, SON OF DAVID, HAVE MERCY ON ME!"*

Jesus heard his cry, stopped in the middle of the road, and called for Bartimaeus to be brought to Him. As he approached, Jesus asked him, "What is it that you want me to do for you?"

Now, notice that Bartimaeus did NOT ask for an explanation of "why" he was born blind. Instead Bartimaeus' reply was short, swift, and much more practical!

He requested, *"Lord, that I might receive my sight."* He said "Lord, I want to see. I want my eyesight back!" But he was saying much more than that! "Lord, I want my eyesight back. I want my vision back. I want my ability to work and make my own living back.

I want my productivity, my potential, and my dignity back. I want my life back!" Then Jesus answered, *"Go thy way, thy faith hath made thee whole."* The Bible says that immediately he received his sight and became a follower of Jesus!

I've learned something from Bartimaeus. It seems that it is more productive to pray for help, than it is to sit in a dusty ditch and ask yourself, "Why?"

To call on the name of Jesus for a miracle, is much more powerful than to question God about the "whys" of life! When given an opportunity to receive from Jesus, Bartimaeus seemed to FORGET about the "whys," instead he PRESSED for "what" he desired from God!

Life is hard enough without us making it harder on ourselves. It seems to me that some of us, for some odd reason, love pain. Surprisingly, it could possibly be a religious thing. There are religions which teach that self inflicted pain is somehow redemptive and justifying. In fact, it is believed by some, "the more pain, the better."

There are people in this world, who make long prayerful pilgrimages on their knees thinking that their pain will pay for their sins. Others, bound by ancient and ignorant forms of heathenism, pierce the flesh of their own backs with huge meat hooks, then tie carts to the hooks with which they pull heavy loads through the streets. They believe that their parade of pain somehow pleases God, as the flesh is agonizingly ripped from their bodies.

Christians also have become masters at self inflicted pain. For instance, we love to continually heap heavy loads of guilt and condemnation on one another, and even on ourselves. Long after God has forgiven us of committed wrongs through our confession of sin and the cleansing power of the blood, we rehearse our disobedience over and over mentally and verbally. This is self inflicted and useless pain.

Some who name the name of Christ gossip, accuse, judge and murder the reputation of others receiving a strange sort of pleasure out of it. Yet, we have been taught repeatedly from the scriptures that when we behave like this, we are sowing a field of pain that we will eventually harvest ourselves. Then, when we reap what we've planted, we whine, cry, groan, and moan, even though we did it to ourselves!

Then there is the age old practice of asking, "Why?" Somehow, we have been convinced that it is somehow supremely spiritual to always ask "Why?" when something particularly painful happens.

. . . *"Why did that automobile accident occur?"*

. . . *"Why did God allow a storm to destroy my home?"*

. . . *"Why did that good person die so tragically?"*

. . . *"Why was my baby born this way?"*

. . . *"Why can't I be better looking?"*

. . . *"Why is the whole world against me?"*

There is no end to the "whys" of life. Life is filled with negatives which cannot be readily explained. Life is hard. Bad things happen to good people. Life certainly is not fair. Now, let me guess. You're probably asking "Why isn't it fair?"

I have a question for you! Why do we always feel compelled to ask "Why?"

To habitually ask why, infers that we believe we can always find the answer. Or perhaps we believe God always owes us an answer. Maybe we believe there's always going to be a specific answer! Is there? I'm not so sure.

Would it be impossible to believe that some things happen . . . just because they happen? No, I'm not saying that anything happens by "chance" or "luck," but I am saying that there are other forces at work in this world other than the power and will of God.

When we think that there is some great divine purpose in all events, we are saying that God somehow is behind everything. This simply is not true. Everything that happens, is not of God! Satan causes some events to occur and nature is the cause of others. Be reminded that nature is corrupt and out of balance due to the sin of man.

Surely, there is a cause for every event, but not always a divine one. The belief that God is in "direct control" of all specific events is an erroneous one. Many today hold to a faulty and perverted view of the "sovereignty of God" in which they believe that God is behind everything that happens. Is this true? I must say, if God is in "control" of everything in this world, then He truly has made a mess!

Everything is not an act of God achieving some mysterious purpose! No matter what your insurance policy says, storms are not necessarily "acts of God." Jesus rebuked storms more than once. Surely He would not have rebuked His own Father's act! This kind of thinking can lock you into an anger against God that has the potential of increasing your pain during hard times. Do we actually love pain that much?

Which is more important, answering the "Whys" of life, or discovering the "Whats," "Wheres," and "Hows" of life? I mean "What are we going to do now that we are in this situation?", "Where are we going now?", and "How are we going to deal with this situation?" Even better, how about asking ourselves, "<u>What</u> does God want me to do in this situation?" "<u>Where</u> is God taking me now?" and "<u>How</u> is God going to solve my present problems?" I believe these are always better questions to ask than "why?"

The Bible teaches a principle which we call the "law of sowing and reaping." All of life follows this principle. Corn seed produces corn, apple seed produces apples, love seed produces love, and financial seed produces finances. This is a governing law of God and it can work for you, or it can work against you!

We can sow bad seed and receive a bad harvest, or we can sow good seed and reap a good harvest. The law of sowing and reaping works, and it works all of the time. However, it is true that not everything that happens in life is a direct result of your sowing.

For instance, we would never say that everything good and positive that ever happened to us was the direct result of our sowing good seed. That would be tantamount to saying that we somehow had something to do with all of our blessings. We would never say such a thing.

We know that God has blessed us by His grace and mercy in ways that we don't deserve. We know that some blessings are pure gifts of grace because we have never sown the seed for such a gift. Right?

If this is true, why do we think that every negative and bad thing that happens is the reaping of some evil seed we have planted? Doesn't it make sense to you that some of the evil that occurs is simply the attack of the devil?

"The thief cometh not but for to steal, and to kill, and to destroy." *John 10:10*

Those are Jesus' words, and He was speaking of the devil. He was teaching us that Satan will attack our lives, just like he attacked Adam and Eve in the garden of Eden.

Did they deserve their attack? Did God have some dark and secret purpose for their attack and temptation? Before you place the blame on God, remember that James said . . .

"Let no man say when he is tempted, I am tempted of God: for God cannot be tempted with evil, neither tempteth he any man."

James 1:13

It is important for you, as a human being, not to automatically judge God as the guilty party every time your life takes a tough turn.

Do you know why? Because the Bible teaches that God is your friend and your Saviour!

You need to be in a right relationship with Him, and not be angry with Him. You cannot be angry with God, and trust in God at the same time!

"For the wrath of man worketh not the righteousness of God."

James 1:20

Trust and faith are principles of righteousness by which we are to live our lives. Without faith we cannot please God![1] In other words, too much asking "Why?" can short circuit your ability to walk with God, and hear from God.

It can also keep you from being clued in by God on the "whats," the "wheres," and the "hows" of life, which are so much more important! Too much asking "Why?" can be detrimental to your faith, which is your key to overcoming in this life.[2]

Did you know that Jesus addressed the "whys?" of life?

"And as Jesus passed by, he saw a man which was blind from his birth. And his disciples asked him saying, Master, who did sin, this man, or his parents, that he was born blind? Jesus answered, Neither hath this man sinned, nor his parents, but that the works of God should be made manifest in him. I must work the works of him that sent me, while it is day: the night cometh, when no man can work. As long as I am in the world, I am the light of the world. When he had

thus spoken, he spat on the ground, and made clay of the spittle, and he anointed the eyes of the blind man with the clay, and said unto him, Go, wash in the pool of Siloam, (which is by interpretation, Sent). He went his way therefore, and washed, and came seeing."

John 9:1-7

When Jesus' disciples asked "Who" had sinned to cause this man to be born blind, they were actually asking "Why is he blind?" The Jews believed that all sickness was a direct result of sin. In other words, they believed that there was always a direct and divine cause for every tragedy in life.

A man so born either had sinning parents, or as they believed, had committed sin himself while still in his mother's womb. Now, to you and I their question may sound ridiculous. However, they are no more ridiculous than we are when we think there is always a "why."

May I also add that our endless questioning of God about "why" certain things have happened in our lives is as futile as trying to figure out what that baby did wrong in his mothers' womb.

Jesus answered their question, yet never told them "why" the man was born blind. Listen to what He said.

"Neither hath this man sinned, nor his parents:"

Now you and I both know that the man and his parents had at some point in life committed sins. What Jesus was saying is that

33

none of them had committed any sins that had directly caused the man's blindness. (This was what the disciples had asked about).

Also, note that at this point Jesus had fully answered their question. The disciples had "assumed" that someone's sin was the cause of the malady. However, Jesus said that a specific personal sin was not the cause, but HE NEVER TOLD THEM WHAT THE CAUSE WAS.

It doesn't look like Jesus thought He owed them a "why" in this case, because Jesus never explained the "why" of the man's blindness. Instead He moves right into the "what," and tells them "what" He is going to do about it.

Realize now that the King James translators added punctuation marks and sentence structure where the original Greek manuscripts make no such distinctions. When Jesus said, *"Neither hath this man sinned nor his parents,"* he had completely answered the disciples' question. In effect, a period could be placed after Jesus' comment. There, Jesus begins a new sentence.

> *" . . . But that the works of God should be made manifest in him . . . I must work the works of him that sent me while it is day . . . "*
>
> *John 9:3b-4a*

Jesus did not say that the man was born blind just so He could heal him. (This would be quite cruel in my thinking. This would lead us to believe that everyone that is <u>not</u> healed of blindness is evidently made blind for the purpose "of <u>not</u> being healed.") Jesus did NOT explain to them why the man was born blind, but rather explained to them WHY HE WAS GOING TO HEAL HIM!

He simply said that He was going to manifest the works of God in the man's life. This infers that Jesus, by no means, considered the man's blindness to be the work of God, but rather the work and will of God was that his eyes be healed.

This is exactly what Jesus did, and called it "the works of God!" The "religious" disciples were trying to theorize about the man's cause of blindness and possible sinfulness. Jesus, on the other hand, was moving toward a positive solution of the man's problem!

Now we have learned something! It is a simple lesson that will alleviate a lot of mental anguish in our lives. "FORGET the past and PRESS toward the future." This is what Jesus did, and this is what Bartimaeus did, and this is what you and I need to do when life gets hard!

GOD'S GOODNESS IS GUARANTEED WHEN YOU . . .

➤ "FORGET AND PRESS"

The Apostle Paul said it wonderfully!
> " . . . *FORGETTING those things which are behind, and reaching forth unto those things which are before, I PRESS toward the mark of the high calling of God in Christ Jesus.*"   *Philippians 3:13-14*

The "whys" are in the past. If there is a "why" that's important or significant for your spiritual progress, God is big enough to reveal it to you! However, much of our asking "Why?" is a waste of time and of spiritual, mental, and emotional energy! Forget the past and move on. Forget past mistakes, forget past sins, forget past regrets, forget past failures, and forget the unexplainable past. Move forward because faith is a forward motion!

Much of our asking "Why?" is in all actuality, an accusation against God. We are asking God why He did this horrible thing to us! God is not to blame for the hard things in life.

Maybe you made a mistake that brought about some of your suffering. (The Bible teaches this. Jonahs' disobedience and Jobs' fears brought hardship into their lives). Be mature enough to face that possibility. If God tells you that the "why" of your negative circumstance is "your fault," then so be it. I would rather discover that I have made a mistake and that I'm responsible than that God has hurled hardship at my life for no purpose.

I need a friend, and if I cannot trust my friend God, who can I trust? If I have made a mistake, I can repent and get myself fixed, but if God has become my enemy and destroyer, how can I change Him? Some say God throws things at us to strengthen and develop us. May I say that the Bible teaches that Satan throws things at us to stop and destroy us!

Once we understand that the hardships we encounter come from our enemy, many "whys?" are automatically answered. But there is something more important than the "whys!"

PRESS TOWARD THE "WHENS," "WHERES," AND "HOWS" THAT WILL BRING TO LIGHT YOUR SOLUTIONS! Don't let the "whys?" get to you. Jesus didn't seem to think the "whys" always mattered.

FORGET and PRESS is your GUARANTEE OF GOD'S GOODNESS!

LIFE IS HARD, BUT REMEMBER, GOD IS GOOD!

Chapter 4

"I THINK GOD LIED TO ME!"

or

What do you do when it seems like God's word just isn't true?

"I thought when I accepted Jesus as my Saviour, that all of my problems would be over!" Many Christians are feeling lied to these days. Well, it is true that Jesus is now solving problems for you, and that you have a new spiritual strength from which to draw. On the other hand, it is also true that you have some new problems such as dealing with Satan, overcoming temptation, maintaining a good example before unbelievers. Oh yes, I almost forgot. There is always that little problem of seemingly unanswered prayer!

I think you know what I'm talking about. You were fellowshipping with a dear brother or sister in the Lord, and you emptied your heart in their lap and they knew just what the Lord would have you to do.

Your Christian friend told you that if you would just pray a certain little prayer that Jesus would ride in on His white steed and rescue you immediately from that problem you've been having. So, you prayed the little prayer, but nothing happened at all! Did God lie to you?

Or maybe it happened like this. You were at church, and like a good church member you listened to your pastor intently, taking notes so as not to miss anything. You carefully noted each principle of success he taught you. You listed each "miracle step" you would need to receive your spiritual breakthrough. Then you did exactly what you were told. Again . . . nothing happened. You are still as defeated as you were to begin with. Did God lie to you?

It could have happened like this. You were praying, and casting all your care over on the Lord, because He cares for you. All of a sudden you heard a voice. "IT'S GOD!", you happily exclaimed. The voice promised you that "such and such" would surely come to pass in your life!

You waited . . . and waited . . . and waited, but it did not happen! Did God lie to you?

Or maybe it happened when you were reading your Bible. You came across an especially exciting and precious promise. You checked it out thoroughly. Sure enough, it was for the New Testament Christian. You decided to believe the promise, claim it as your own by faith, and receive the benefit of it.

Again . . . nothing happened! Did God lie to you?

May I share something with you that will be liberating, life-giving, and save you from a lot of heartache as you walk with Jesus, fight the fight of faith, and lay hold on eternal life? "Someone" may lie to you. **BUT GOD CANNOT!**

"God, . . . cannot lie,"   *Titus 1:2*

This must become a settled issue in your heart and mind if you are ever going to be able to fully trust the Lord with your day to day life. That is where you confront hard times, in day to day life! Life is hard, but I remind you GOD IS GOOD!

However, God would not be good if He were able to lie to you. This is the whole issue, "God is good," the Bible declares, therefore *"He cannot lie!"* We must come to a place in our convictions where we are convinced of God's integrity!

We must believe that God is a God of His word and begin to believe that He says what He means and means what He says! This is absolute truth. The entire Christian faith, yes your entire eternity and salvation rests on this fact. *"God cannot lie!"*

Salvation is by faith. Faith is based on God's Word. If God's Word is found to be in error, then we are yet in our sins, and all hope of salvation and eternity in Heaven is gone! "GOD CANNOT LIE!"

May I suggest that we look elsewhere for our problem?

First of all, remember that you, your Christian friends, and even your pastor are all finite, imperfect, problematic, subject to failure, human beings. However, God is infinite, perfect, problem free, and has never failed at anything! If there is a problem, IT MUST BE ON THE HUMAN SIDE of things, not God's. Make sense?

Your Christian friends can make mistakes. Your pastor can fail to teach you "everything" you need to know. And you . . . yeah, let's talk about you for a minute. I suppose you could never be deceived by a "spiritual voice" you heard while in prayer, right?

"Well, I thought that if I was in prayer, the devil couldn't touch me!", you may reply defensively. Oh really?

Jesus was in prayer when He went through His greatest temptations and opportunities for deception.

(Check it out in the gospels where Jesus prayed for forty days at the beginning of His ministry, and again in the garden of Gethsemane just before His death on the cross).

The difference between Jesus and us is that Jesus always used God's Word to test and resist every demonic suggestion. Jesus trusted God's Word totally in such times of hardship. Jesus was convinced that *"GOD CANNOT LIE!"*

Here is a lesson which will help you continually receive God's goodness and mercy in your life. Jesus Himself said it in *Mark 11:22.* *"Have faith in God."*

GOD'S GOODNESS IS GUARANTEED WHEN YOU ...

To have faith in God, literally means to "hold" faith in God. You are created to be a "faith holder." Your heart is a faith container. Allow faith to be contained there.

"Faith cometh by hearing (understanding) and hearing (understanding) by the Word of God."

Romans 10:17

I think God lied to me!

If you have faith in God then you must not blame God when you experience "prayer failure."

Maybe . . . what you prayed for is not really promised in the Bible.

Maybe . . . you prayed unscripturally in some way.

Maybe . . . you tried to pray past someone's free will.
(This is spiritual trespassing)

Maybe . . . you prayed amiss, or to consume upon your own lusts.

Maybe . . . you are not living in the light you've been given.

Maybe . . . you heard a deceiving voice.

Maybe . . . you really did not believe when you prayed.

Maybe . . . you allowed doubt into your heart after you prayed.

Maybe . . . you have been misinformed.

Maybe . . . you have misunderstood some things.

Maybe . . . you really don't fathom the Father's great love for you.

Maybe . . . your answer has not manifested "yet," but is on its way on Angel's wings!

Maybe . . . a lot of things.

We are imperfect. We do not know it all. Maybe we should admit that God is never our problem, but that our problem is most often "us."

Now, I love you Christian brother or sister. I'm trying to help you here, but I can only help you with "truth" for it's the truth that makes us free.[1]

It seems to me that if there is a mistake being made, we would rather recognize that WE are making it somewhere here on planet Earth. Surely the problem is not in Heaven! If I have a problem, I can repent. If God does, then we're sunk!

God is Good! Don't allow tragedy to transform your theology. Don't let your life experience (which is but a vapor) cancel out the veracity of God's Word (which is forever settled in Heaven). No matter what we feel, see, hear, or experience, God's Word is true and accurate! HAVE FAITH IN GOD!

Think about this for a moment. What if twenty people responded to your pastor's evangelistic invitation next Sunday. Let's imagine that they "walked the aisle," stated that they desired to be born again, and prayed the sinner's prayer with your pastor. Let's even say they all participated in water baptism that same evening.

Then let's imagine that one month later we did a little research, checked up on those twenty people, and found that not one of them was living a righteous lifestyle. Some of them were getting drunk. Some were committing fornication. Others were lying and cheating.

Now, let me ask you. Would this prove that salvation is not real? Would it prove that God did not desire to save them? Would it prove that your pastor was a false prophet? Finally, would it prove that God refused to answer their prayer?

The answer to all of the above is an absolute and resounding, No!

May I suggest that it proves one thing only. Somehow, I don't know how and you don't know how, but somehow, those twenty people did not receive the miracle of salvation! I don't know what the problem was, but I know what it was not. THE PROBLEM WAS NOT GOD! HE IS THE SOLUTION OF ALL PROBLEMS. HE IS NEVER THE PROBLEM!

Just because someone prayed for healing and did not receive it, proves nothing about God's will in the matter. We cannot let experience interpret the Bible.

We must begin to let the Bible interpret our experience. When we learn to do this, OUR EXPERIENCE WILL BEGIN TO REFLECT THE BIBLE!

Just because someone thought that God led them to start a business, and it failed, does not prove or disprove anything about God's will to prosper His people! Don't let your experience interpret the Bible. HAVE FAITH IN GOD!

The Bible is full of the testimonies of people who DID get saved, DID get healed, DID get delivered, DID prosper, and DID receive answers to prayer.

This is still the will of God. HAVE FAITH IN GOD!

When you are tempted to think that God's promise is not true, . remember that God's Word is more true than your experience. God's Word is more true than your feelings, your thinking, and your analysis of the results. Learn to trust in the God that cannot lie!

LIFE IS HARD my friend,

but always remember, GOD IS GOOD . . .

and, HE CANNOT LIE!

Chapter 5

"I DON'T HAVE AN INFERIORITY COMPLEX, I'M JUST INFERIOR!"

or

What do you do when you feel like a failure?

So, you failed! Oh, it goes farther than that? You always fail? Have you become convinced that you're a failure and you'll always be a failure? I am an expert in failure myself!

I don't want to share too many explicit details, but let's just say that even though I was raised in church as a child, I failed morally during my teens and early twenties. I've also failed at work. I've failed at providing for my family. I've failed at business. I've failed God. I've failed in ministry. I've failed in loving my wife. I've failed in the romance department. I've failed in training my children. My list goes on and on. If you are interested, we could compare lists sometime. Believe me, I know what it feels like to be FROZEN IN FAILURE!

The Bible records the lives of several failures. Adam was the original human failure. Several are mentioned who were frozen in failure and never thawed out! Cain was one, Saul another, and Absolom another. Of course, the ultimate failure was Judas. Failures exist. But they did not have to fail, and you don't either!

All of those failures had one thing in common. They were quitters! They stopped. They chucked it in. They threw in the towel. They got mad, took their ball, and went home! Do you hear what I'm saying? Only quitters are true failures! Have you quit?

If you have quit, you can start again. I've found the cure for failing! It's called LEARNING! Please, let me show you. Jesus taught us about learning instead of failing!

"Then said Jesus to those Jews which believed on him, IF YE CONTINUE IN MY WORD, then ARE YE my DISCIPLES, indeed; and YE SHALL KNOW THE TRUTH, and the TRUTH SHALL MAKE YOU FREE."   *John 8:31-32*

Your attitude will determine your altitude in life. You need to get off of the "failure in life" thing and begin to believe that you are a "learner!" You are not a failure, but a learner! Jesus said that if we would CONTINUE in His word, then we are His DISCIPLES.

A disciple is a follower, a pupil, or literally a LEARNER. If you will not quit, but continue, then Jesus calls you a "LEARNER." You cannot be a FAILURE if you will be a FOLLOWER, because Jesus is the greatest SUCCESS in history!

". . . a just man falleth seven times, and riseth up again"   *Proverbs 24:16*

A just man, a godly man, a man who is FOLLOWING Jesus, gets back up when he falls down. WINNERS fall like everyone else . . . they just get back up!

"QUITTERS ARE FAILURES!
but . . .
LEARNERS ARE WINNERS!"

I don't have an inferiority complex, I'm just inferior!

Jesus taught us not to quit, but to learn, and by learning we are made free from failure. YOU DON'T HAVE TO BE FROZEN IN FAILURE! YOU CAN BECOME FREE FROM FAILURE BY BECOMING A LEARNER!

GOD'S GOODNESS IS GUARANTEED WHEN YOU . . .

> ➤ **DECIDE TO BE A LEARNER INSTEAD OF A FAILURE**

"Without faith it is impossible to PLEASE him: for he that cometh to God must BELIEVE that he is, and that he is a REWARDER of them that diligently SEEK him."

Hebrews 11:6

"God seekers" are "GOD PLEASERS!" And God REWARDS GOD SEEKERS! Listen to me, IF YOU DON'T QUIT . . . YOU WIN!

Keep on seeking God. If you fall down then get back up! It's a learning situation. Just keep falling forward. Get up and go again. Don't stop! Don't quit! Seek God! He's pleased with your attitude of seeking, learning, and following! TRUST GOD TO STRENGTHEN YOU AND JUST KEEP ON FOLLOWING!

Don't look back! Jesus told us to, *"Remember Lot's wife."* [1] She looked back. She quit! She was frozen in failure.

God loves a learner. His attitude is one of mercy and compassion toward His children who have their hearts set on success even though they make many mistakes. I believe a GOD SEEKER is a GOD PLEASER! You don't have to be successful for God to love you or believe in you! You're His child. He loves you just because you are born into the family.

I heard about a man who invited his pastor to a little league football game where his son was playing. The proud father and his pastor watched every play carefully. They didn't want to miss it if the boy got a chance to carry the ball. Finally the football was handed off to the young athlete. After securing the ball firmly in both hands he started to move to the right.

Seeing his opponents closing in on him, he started to move back toward the left. There were more of them. In a split second he was lying under a huge pile of youngsters with arms and legs flying everywhere!

The boy had not moved the football even one yard. The pastor figured that the dad would be disappointed. Instead, the man was shouting, "Did you see that, did you see that?" "See what?", asked the pastor. The proud father shouted back, "Did you see those two good moves he made?"

God sees those "two good moves you made" just before you got tackled! He's proud of you for trying! You're His child. He loves you! And He is thrilled when you won't quit!

The Bible tells us about those who wouldn't quit. They all won battles, experienced success, and became winners with God.

Moses succeeded at age eighty after failing at forty! Samson received his anointing back and defeated the godless Philistines after a moral failure. Paul succeeded in faith and ministry after being a zealous persecutor and murderer of Christians.

Peter won multiplied thousands of people to Jesus Christ while preaching before multitudes, only days after denying Jesus in front of a handful of people! FOLLOWERS OF JESUS ARE NOT FAILURES! DON'T QUIT . . . LEARN! DON'T STOP . . . FOLLOW!

Thomas Edison learned the secret of "LEARNING." Edison dedicated forty years to the development of the incandescent light bulb. He than discovered that the element had a life of only forty-five hours. Edison experimented with some six thousand organic materials before he found one that would boost the burning time up to one thousand hours.

After five thousand tries someone asked him if he was discouraged somewhat by his failures. He wasn't at all! In fact he replied, "I've found five thousand things that will not work." Edison was much too involved in LEARNING to become involved in FAILING! As long as you are learning, you are NEVER FAILING!

Friend, you may have failed, but as long as you are following Jesus, you are not a failure. YOU ARE A LEARNER! And after you have learned you will succeed! You may be in the "School of Hard Knocks," but at least you're still in school. Yes, life is hard, but remember, **GOD IS GOOD!**

Chapter 6

"I JUST CAN'T TAKE IT ANYMORE!"

or

What do you do when life just gets to be too much?

There are only twenty-four hours in a day. Many believers I know easily fill all of them. By the time we work all day, do our chores at home, give a little time to volunteer work or ministry, have some family time, run our errands, deliver our kids to all of their games, practices, meetings, parties, and over night stays, and get perhaps five to seven hours of sleep, there is not a whole lot of time left. Oh! I forgot to mention prayer and Bible study! Many Christians forget those too. In fact, more forget these items than don't, and they forget them daily!

Then life begins to pour in. And remember, "life is hard!" Our lives would be hectic enough, but then add a sufficient amount of evil every day and it really gets to be "hard!" Your neighbor blows up because your son's baseball bat went through his side window. "No, not his baseball, his bat!"

Then Sister Sue calls your wife and fills her ears with the latest church gossip. Now your wife is either mad or depressed. A bill collector calls because you haven't paid your bill. You haven't paid your bills because you haven't had time to balance your checkbook. You promise to get the check in the next day. Now you will have to spend three hours at your desk tonight.

The grass you were going to mow will just have to wait! Aaaaagggghhhh!!! What is that??? Your wife has burst into tears! She runs into the bedroom. After about thirty minutes of begging her

53

to tell you what in the world is wrong, she informs you that you are ignoring her! Sound familiar?

Add to all of this the financial pressure, the sales pressure, the social pressure, the in-law pressure, and all of the emotional pressures of living in today's world and you begin to understand why people are coming apart mentally, maritally, and spiritually.

If you include bankruptcy, fatal diseases, car accidents, substance abuse, and various other problems in on top of everything else, life gets to be extremely hard!

I guess the only thing I would like to add to the picture I have just painted is to tell you that I am a pastor, and I do well to have two free evenings at home a week. Thankfully, I don't have many of the pressures I just mentioned but I do spend a lot of time ministering to people who do. I deal with these types of problems every day. So if you are living the life I just described, I can sympathize with you!

Sometimes you feel like giving up. You would quit your job if it would do any good. You would give up your house which you don't have time to paint, if you had anywhere else to live. You may feel like there is no escape outside of suicide. And you know that is a sin, however suicide even seduces some Christians.

Alcoholism gets others. Adultery gets more. One of these might get you unless you learn how to cope with life when it gets to be too much!

GOD IS GOOD! Surely He has a way to help us deal with the pressures. Certainly one secret is found in *1 Peter 5:7*.

"Casting all your care upon him; for he careth for you."

I could say quite a few things about the spiritual principle of casting all of your cares upon the Lord. We are not designed to handle the pressures of life without His help. He has huge shoulders. Learn to trust Him. Learn to pray and leave the burden of your problems with Him. He does care about you, and He will care for you, if you will let Him.

I want to give you some additional Biblical advice that is practical. Some believers have over spiritualized their "casting their care on the Lord" and don't ever do anything practical about their problem. It's like the person who prays to God for financial needs to be met, but refuses to work. It just won't produce the needed results!

GOD IS GOOD! He has some principles that will help you when placed into action in your life. I want to share a powerful one with you!

GOD'S GOODNESS IS GUARANTEED WHEN YOU . . .

➤ "PRIORITIZE AND ENERGIZE"

One of the greatest thieves of spiritual, mental, and physical energy is wrong priorities! Do you want the energy to handle life at its worst? Then you must learn to "PRIORITIZE AND ENERGIZE."

Here is a list of your responsibilities in life, prioritized according to God's order as taught in the Bible:

1. God

2. Spouse

3. Children

4. Education

5. Ministry

6. Career

By properly prioritizing these six areas of responsibility you can enjoy the richest measure of God's grace, strength, and help. I will explain from the scriptures.

GOD IS TO BE FIRST and foremost in your life. You must love Him above all else, obey Him above all else, and give yourself to Him above all else.

> *". . . Thou shalt love the Lord thy God with all thy heart, and with all thy soul, and with all thy mind. This is the first and great commandment."*
>
> *Matthew 22:37-38*

In order to cope with life, you must have God's grace, strength, help, favor, and power. There is only one place to receive these things, from Him! You must go to Him directly! This is why Jesus came and died for us, to bring us close to God the Father. We can now fellowship with Him and receive His divine influence. God can ENERGIZE you for living.

You were never created to live or operate independently from God. You were designed to be UTTERLY DEPENDENT upon Him. Therefore, when anything . . . <u>anything</u> becomes more important to us than God, we are out of balance, out of divine order, and have perverted priorities. Trouble is on the way! By the way, preachers and church leaders, please do not confuse ministry with God! Ministry is further down the list. God Himself is number one. We are to give ourselves to the Lord of the work, not just to the work of the Lord!

If God is NUMBER ONE in your life, you will spend time with Him in PRAYER and FELLOWSHIP. If God is number one, you will allow Him to TALK to you through His WORD. Your wife or husband would not believe you love them if you never wanted to be alone with them. Neither would God.

YOUR SPOUSE COMES SECOND in your order of priorities.

> *"And the second (commandment) is like unto it, Thou shalt love thy neighbor as thyself."*
>
> *Matthew 22:39*

A neighbor is someone near; a near friend. No one is to be as near to you as your spouse. Your spouse is more important to you than your children. Children are to separate from their parents eventually and be joined to their own spouses.[1] The child rearing years of parenthood are limited in number. But marriage is until "death do you part!" There is a strength, an ENERGY, to be derived from the marriage relationship that cannot be found in any other. God instituted and gave marriage to mankind because it was not good for man to be alone.[2]

Your husband or wife must come before ministry, career, or any other responsibility. Great power is infused into people's lives when they obey the Apostle Paul's directives.

"Husbands, love your wives, even as Christ also loved the church, and gave himself for it."

Ephesians 5:25

". . . and the wife see that she reverence her husband."

Ephesians 5:33

I believe that Paul here, touched on the greatest needs in the male and female personalities. The greatest social and emotional need of a woman, is to be loved and valued by her husband. Jesus loved and valued the church enough to lay His own life down for it. A woman longs to feel cherished, protected, and precious to her husband.

Great ENERGY for living is imparted when the husband fulfills this need. A husband is to give time, attention, and care to his wife. He must be willing to lay things down for her. His life must become hers if she is to "feel loved!"

The greatest social and emotional need of a man, is to be honored, respected, and looked up to, by his wife. There is something about the male personality that longs to be honored and respected by his wife. When she brags on her man, or honors him, he gets bigger and bigger on the inside. Behind most great men, there are great women!

Much of the time, adulterous affairs are birthed out of emotional rather than sexual lust. When a person is not meeting the emotional needs of their mate, someone else may be sought, either consciously or unconsciously, to meet them. If another person notices your spouse, and begins to meet unmet emotional needs, he or she could be led like a lamb to the slaughter! Please, believe me. Your marriage is a high priority in life.

God gave you to one another so that you could help, aid, and assist one another. You have the ability to make one another strong emotionally! Do it! The Bible says that the man who finds a wife, finds a good thing.[3] Sacrificially love your wife, sir. She will bless and ENERGIZE your life.

YOUR CHILDREN ARE THIRD. They are more important than your job. They are more important than your ministry. They are certainly more important than your hobbies. Love them. Train them. Discipline them. Educate them.[4] Children are a blessing from the Lord.[5] This means that they are to bless and ENERGIZE your life.[6] If you do not invest in them however, they have the ability to break your heart and deenergize your life as well.

YOUR EDUCATION IS FOURTH. Before you can be effective at any trade or profession, you must have some degree of training. You understand that, but do you understand that you also need to be educated in the things of God? He is your number one priority. Serving God is not quite as easy as falling off of a log! It demands a focused effort. Likewise, you need to be taught about marriage and family relationships. This is why we read the Bible, attend church, and receive teaching and Christian discipleship. Education ENERGIZES you for all of your other responsibilities, including ministry and career.

YOUR MINISTRY IS FIFTH. No one can adequately deal with life without maturity. And maturity cannot be attained without also being involved in ministry. We are created to be SERVANTS! I didn't say employees, I said servants! God created you to serve Him, an invisible God, and believe by faith that His blessing will compensate you! People of faith will serve. Servants with faith receive blessings in life that are far beyond what others receive. In the day of judgment, we will not be rewarded for our hours on the job, but for our MINISTRY and SERVICE!

Through ministry and service we learn to help others, we learn to be thankful, we learn to interact with and love people. Many valuable lessons of life are learned. In addition, the fulfillment of accomplishment is enjoyed!

Every Christian should be a servant in the local church, supporting the vision of their pastor, cooperating with ministry teams to reach their city and the world for Christ. The purpose of life is to love God and people!

If you really love God and if you really love people, you will become involved in the "Father's business" of "getting God and people together through ministry!"

Now, some may doubt that ministry should come ahead of career. Consider the following verse of scripture.

> *". . . let him labor, working with his hands the thing which is good, that he may have to give to him that needeth."*
>
> *Ephesians 4:28*

God's Word says that the reason we work and earn is not for the purpose of wealth accumulation and not for emotional or egotistical fulfillment but rather for the purpose of financing our ministry. The purpose for your personal financial wealth is to finance and pay for your personal assignment from God. This is what Jesus used His money for! You see, we exist on this planet to have a relationship with God, to glorify Him, and to obey Him.

Presently, there is a warfare between God and His enemy. Our assignment therefore, includes assisting in that warfare between GOOD and EVIL. You will surely win your own warfare over evil if you will serve and help others!

Oh yes! And how are you to be fulfilled in life? Well it is not by climbing the corporate ladder or even earning your first million dollars. Rather it is found in your relationship with God, your service to Him, and your accomplishments for "His" glory and praise!

You will be much more fulfilled in ministry than career for your career is temporal and your ministry has eternal ramifications!

Your choice then is between the temporary fulfillment of worldly accomplishment or the eternal fulfillment of Heavenly accomplishment.

YOUR CAREER OR JOB IS SIXTH. By no means is your life's work unimportant. You must invest into it and do it heartily as unto the Lord. It is inseparably tied to your ministry for your ministry is supported by your vocation. And of course, you are to be a witness for Jesus Christ within and through that chosen vocation.

TAKE A LOOK AT YOUR RELATIONSHIPS! Every relationship in your life affects you to some degree. Discern how much of your investment they truly deserve by measuring their effect upon your priorities. Perhaps some of your relationships will have to be abandoned.

Satan will attempt to send time wasters and dream killers into your life. I try to invest time with only those people who I am helping or who are really helping me! Critics deserve little of my time. I reserve my best time for my family and friends.

PRIORITIZE AND ENERGIZE! Do it! Divine strength will come to your life as you bring divine balance to your involvements. You will probably find that there are some things in your life that will have to be limited, or even cut out entirely. PROPER PRIORITIZA-TION demands that you survey your activities and categorize them correctly. God will give you wisdom in this.

Some things can only be done by you. For instance, you need recreation and physical exercise. No one can do these things for you. They are important if you are to remain healthy and glorify God in your body and mind. Likewise, you who are parents cannot abdicate your role to others. You must parent your children, for God gave them to <u>you</u>!

Some things which you are doing however, may possibly be done by someone else. The only way to increase the amount of time you have is by borrowing or buying someone else's. If your life is going to be prioritized and balanced you must learn to DELEGATE! FIND someone to do what you are not particularly good at or what you do not have to do personally.

If you have the finances but no time to clean your home or mow your lawn, HIRE someone to do it for you. DISTRIBUTE household chores fairly among all of your family members! If your volunteer work at Church is consuming too much time, RECRUIT helpers into your ministry! GET some help! The FRUSTRATION you save, the LIFE you save, and the SOUL you save, may be your own!

Cast all of your cares upon the Lord. Then PRIORITIZE AND ENERGIZE. **Life is hard . . . but God really, really is GOOD! HE WILL HELP YOU. THROUGH HIS GOODNESS, YOU CAN LEARN TO HANDLE LIFE!**

Chapter 7

"I'M QUITE SURE . . . THIS IS YOUR 491st TIME!"

or

How do you forgive when it seems impossible?

One Sunday after church, a woman walked up to me with one of the biggest smiles I had ever seen in my life! "Thank you, Pastor David," she said. "You don't know how much your teaching has helped me. For the first time in years, I have peace in my heart. Now I'm sure of my salvation. I'm so happy! Thank you for teaching me HOW TO FORGIVE!"

This woman had received a powerful miracle! She had been emotionally healed from a devastating heartbreak she had suffered many years before. Let me share her story with you, because I think it will help you.

She and her husband both worked, so they hired a babysitter to help care for their children. The kids adored the young lady and she quickly became part of the family. In fact, the woman and her babysitter became close friends. One day the woman came home from work only to find that the babysitter and her husband had run away together.

Her heart was more than broken. It was shattered in a million pieces. "How could her husband desert her and their children like this?", she thought. "How could her young friend, who had been like her own sister, so heartlessly steal her husband and her children's father?"

Her initial shock was followed by grief, and then feelings of rejection, anger and hatred. Emotionally crushed, she couldn't seem to control her feelings at all! She began to focus her hatred primarily toward the young lady who had stolen her husband and broken up her home. Her hatred became bitterness, a bitterness which she harbored in her heart for many years.

Being a Christian, this woman had been taught that she was to forgive those who had wronged her. But how could she forgive this? This was impossible to forgive! At least, it seemed impossible until the day I pointed out to her that *"all things are possible to him that believeth."*[1]

You see, Jesus not only taught us to forgive people who sin against us, He also taught us HOW! Almost every Christian understands that he is to forgive people their trespasses, but many do not understand how to accomplish this task.

Many times over the years, I have taught people how to forgive others when it seems impossible. I always try to help people understand what true forgiveness is. I have been amazed at what I've found.

After I teach, I will lead the congregation in a prayer inviting the Holy Spirit to search their hearts and reveal any unforgiveness or bitterness that might be there.

Without fail, more than half of the people will lift their hands indicating that God has shown them some type of unforgiveness toward others. This is quite alarming to me!

Think about it. If more than 50 percent of all believers are holding on to unforgiveness, is it any wonder that they are spiritually weak? Is it any wonder why Christians suffer under a debilitating weight of guilt and condemnation?

Does this have anything to do with the constant problems we have in the church with strife, division, and confusion? Could this possibly hinder the Church in its mission and maybe even stop us from fulfilling the great commission given to us by the Lord Jesus?

This woman was thrilled. Not only did I uncompromisingly teach her that she must forgive the young lady who had sinned against her (as well as her husband who had since died), I went one giant step further. I also taught her from the Bible HOW to do it! Jesus taught us how to forgive and this is what I desire to share with you!

This precious woman told me that after I taught her how to forgive, she realized her responsibility before God. Desiring to please Him and to be free from her hatred, she acted on what she had heard by faith. She forgave the woman who had stolen her husband and broken her heart. She also wrote the woman a letter to let her know that she was forgiven. She told the woman that she had been taught how to forgive at church. Her letter was compassionate and loving.

Surprisingly, the babysitter wrote back and repented for what she had done and believe it or not, they began to build their friendship again! They became pen pals! Wow! GOD REALLY IS GOOD! "Pastor David," she said, "I have my friend back. I know I'm saved. And I have peace in my heart for the first time in years." She was thrilled and so was I. I believe that our Father in Heaven was thrilled too!

Terrible things happen to people. Life just isn't fair. People are murdered, raped, robbed, rejected, hurt, and lied about. Sins are committed against people which seemingly are impossible to forgive! Yet as Christians, we are commanded by our Lord Jesus to forgive freely and completely.

I say freely and completely because some people try to play games with this issue of forgiveness.

Some will not forgive until the person who offended them personally or publicly repents,[1] suffers in some manner, or begs for forgiveness. They desire to make the offender somehow earn their forgiveness!

[1](While it is true that Jesus taught us to forgive when one who sins against us repents, there are other passages where Jesus taught us to forgive without any repentance on the part of the offending person. Forgiving this person is important for our spiritual benefit as I will point out later).

Many people will say, "I can forgive, but I can never forget." While I agree that we may not be able to totally erase the offense from our physical memory banks, we certainly cannot justify meditating upon it or becoming obsessed with it in our thinking either!

If we insist on the right to "rehearse the curse," it will curse us and perhaps even "hearse" us in the end!

It is senseless to allow these things to continue to devastate our lives. Let's learn how to forgive! Let's learn to forgive by faith!

GOD'S GOODNESS IS GUARANTEED WHEN WE . . .

➤ "FORGIVE BY FAITH"

"Therefore is the kingdom of heaven likened unto a certain king, which would take account of his servants. And when he had begun to reckon, one was brought unto him, which owed him ten thousand talents. But forasmuch as he had not to pay, his lord commanded him to be sold, and his wife, and children, and all that he had, and payment to be made. The servant therefore fell down, and worshiped him, saying, Lord, have patience with me, and I will pay thee all. Then the Lord of that servant was moved with compassion, and loosed him, and forgave him the debt. But the same servant went out, and found one of his fellowservants, which owed him an hundred pence: and he laid hands on him, and took him by the throat, saying, Pay me that thou owest. And his fellowservant fell down at his feet, and besought him, saying, Have patience with me, and I will pay thee all. And he would not: but went and cast him into prison, till he should pay the debt. So when his fellowservants saw what he had done, they were very sorry, and came and told unto their lord all that was done. Then his lord, after that he had called him, and said unto him, O thou wicked servant, I forgave thee all that debt, because thou desirest me: Shouldest not thou also have had compassion on thy fellowservant,

*even as I had pity on thee? And his lord was wroth,
and delivered him to the tormentors, till he should pay
all that was due unto him. So likewise shall my
heavenly Father do also unto you, if ye from your
hearts forgive not every one his brother their trespasses."*   *Matthew* 18:23-35

Jesus taught us to forgive and why we must forgive, in this story called the "Parable of the Unmerciful Servant." A servant owed his king a large sum of money. One source of reference says it was approximately ten million dollars. The man could not pay what he owed and begged for mercy from the king. The king, moved with compassion, freely and completely forgave the man of the huge debt.

Later, the same man who was forgiven of the ten million dollar debt was also owed two thousand dollars by another man. He went and found that man and demanded immediate payment. This man begged for mercy but the forgiven man would not forgive his debtor! In fact he had the man thrown into prison.

When news of the forgiven mans' lack of mercy reached the king, he became very angry and reversed his former decision. At this point the previously forgiven man was sent to prison and to the tormentors. (Prisons in those days had tormentors instead of softball teams).

It was a dreadful thing to be in prison and to be delivered to the tormentors. Then Jesus made a statement that should cause anyone to shudder with fear. *"So likewise shall my heavenly father do also unto you, if ye from your hearts forgive not every one his brother their trespasses."*

Did you hear what Jesus said? He has told us that God the Father, our King, reserves the right to reverse the decision on our forgiveness. He has forgiven us of all of our sins symbolized by the ten million dollar debt. Every one of us owed a debt to God, too large to pay. God was merciful to us and forgave us freely and completely! However He can reverse our forgiveness, and deliver us to the "tormentors" if we refuse to forgive others of their sins against us!

The tormentors here represent Satan and unclean spirits who have the ability to torment us with bitterness, depression, anger, hatred, murder, suicide, addiction, disease, pain, and many other forms of human suffering.

There is no protection over our lives from these torments if we refuse to forgive. This is why we MUST forgive. It is for our own good, our peace, health, and our relationship with God.

". . . forgive if ye have ought against any: that your Father also which is in heaven may forgive you your trespasses. But IF YE DO NOT FORGIVE, NEITHER WILL YOUR FATHER WHICH IS IN HEAVEN FORGIVE YOUR TRESPASSES."

Mark 11:25-26

The torment that Jesus mentions could also mean something else:

Hell!

I know that didn't "go over" with you. It doesn't "go over" with hardly anyone, but it's the truth. If you are going to make it through a hard life, I'm afraid you will have to hear some hard truths!

Jesus said that if we will not forgive, God will not forgive us. Unforgiven people do not go to Heaven when they die. They go to Hell.

Jesus said that we must forgive everyone FROM OUR HEARTS! "All right," you say. "How?" Let's allow Jesus to disciple us in this important subject.

> *"Then said he unto his disciples, It is impossible but that offences will come: but woe unto him, through whom they come! It were better for him that a mill-stone were hanged about his neck, and he cast into the sea, than that he should offend one of these little ones. Take heed to yourselves: if thy brother trespass against thee, rebuke him; and if he repent, forgive him. And if he trespass against thee seven times in a day, and seven times in a day turn again to thee, saying, I repent; thou shalt forgive him. And the apostles said unto the Lord, Increase our faith. And the Lord said, If ye had faith as a grain of mustard seed, ye might say unto this sycamine tree, Be thou plucked up by the root, and be thou planted in the sea; and it should obey you."*   Luke 17:1-6

Jesus said that you cannot live life without offenses coming your way. Someone is going to sin against you. But He said, *"Woe unto him, through whom they (the offenses) come!"* Note that the offense does not come from the person, but THROUGH the person. (The Greek word used by Jesus here is "dia" meaning "a channel.")

If it does not come from the person who sins, who did it come FROM? It came from Satan! He is the enemy of your soul. He is the one who desires to wreck your life. He inspires all evil either directly or indirectly! We must learn to blame Satan for our hurts in life and pray for those he uses as his channels. And he often uses them unwittingly. Perhaps we should pray like Jesus, *"Father, forgive them for they know not what they do.[2]"*

The word "offense" means a snare or a trap. This reveals why Satan inspires someone to sin against us. It is a trap! You see, Satan not only wants to curse the offender with judgment from God, he wants to injure you with the initial hurt, rejection, lie, attack, rape, robbery, etc.

He is also setting a trap of unforgiveness for you which will open a spiritual door to torment you throughout your entire life . . . and eternity if possible.

When we take the bait, we are hurting OURSELVES. Friend, your unforgiveness and bitterness will never affect the one who hurt you. He is already judged for his sin against you, and possibly is living in great guilt and condemnation over his act even now! But your continued unforgiveness will continue to torment YOU until you free yourself and your heart completely from it.

Jesus said that the person through whom the offense comes will surely be judged but . . . you "take heed to yourselves." He said, "TAKE CARE OF YOURSELF!" and "PAY ATTENTION TO YOURSELF!" If someone sins against you seven times in one day and repents every time, forgive him.

Another passage says we are to forgive someone seventy times seven, and it mentions no condition of repentance in the person sinning. No, you cannot stop on their 491st sin. Seventy times seven represents an infinite number of offenses. *Love never takes account of the wrongs done to it.*[3]

Jesus' point is this. If the person repents personally to you, compassionately communicate with him. Work out the problem in your relationship. However, the bottom line is this. You must forgive him, even if he sins against you seven times in one day. At this point you might begin to doubt the sincerity of his repentance.

It can be very difficult to continue to forgive a person who repeatedly commits the same sin against you and who repeatedly begs for forgiveness. At this point, something occurred to the Apostles.

"If we are to forgive so freely and completely . . . well then Jesus, increase our faith." The apostles realized that this kind of forgiveness would have to be supernatural for it would be impossible for a human being to accomplish!

It will have to be done by FAITH. I believe this was what Jesus meant when He said that we are to forgive from our HEARTS.

Certainly, we must be sincere when we forgive, but we must do it BY FAITH! *Romans 10:10* says that *"WITH THE HEART MAN BELIEVETH."* You cannot forgive all trespasses and sins simply by an act of your human will.

Some things are so terrible, you will need the miracle power of God to empower you to forgive. You will have to do it by FAITH, for faith is how you tap into God's power!

This is why Jesus said, *"If you had faith as a grain of mustard seed, ye might say unto this sycamine tree, be thou plucked up by the root and be thou planted in the sea; and it should obey you."* Faith is like a seed.

You sow seed. And you say faith. You sow faith by saying it. (See also *Mark 11:23*) Jesus said to release your faith through your words. If you are holding on to unforgiveness, there is a tree growing in your heart and life. It has a root, and that root's name is bitterness.

> *"Follow peace with all men, and holiness, without which no man shall see the Lord: Looking diligently lest any man fail of the grace of God; lest any ROOT OF BITTERNESS springing up TROUBLE YOU, and thereby many are DEFILED."*   Hebrews 12:14-15

The root of bitterness brings trouble to people. We are told that it defiles (spiritually soils) many. The root is best not allowed to grow in us at all

This is possible through immediate forgiveness. But if we find unforgiveness and bitterness in our heart we must act by faith. Those fiery darts of hurt will produce poison in our spiritual system if allowed to remain in us.

Bitterness literally means poison. If a soldier on the battle-field had been pierced with an arrow, and that arrow was not removed, the soldier would eventually die of blood poisoning if not by bleeding. Unforgiveness and bitterness must be removed from your life to avoid spiritual blood poisoning!

We must command unforgiveness to be plucked up and cast out of our hearts by the root. In other words, it must be removed

ALONG WITH THE ROOT of bitterness that is attached to it. Like a dandelion in your yard, you must get the root to stop the trouble! It must be cast in the same sea of forgetfulness that God threw all of your sins into! You do it by faith. FORGIVE BY FAITH!

I invite you to find a quiet place and pray this simple prayer, listening for God to bring the names or faces of people you have not yet forgiven, into your consciousness.

> *Dear Father in Heaven,*
> *Turn the search light of your Spirit upon my heart.*
> *See if there is any unforgiveness or bitterness in me*
> *for anyone, living or dead!*
> *In Jesus' Name, Amen.*

If you have discovered unforgiveness in your heart, pray this prayer by faith:

> *Dear Father in Heaven,*
> *I repent for my unforgiveness and bitterness. I ask*
> *you to forgive me and cleanse me by the blood of*
> *Jesus my Saviour! I choose to forgive*
> *_______________ by faith! I don't blame them, but I*
> *blame Satan who was attacking my life. I forgive the*
> *one through whom the offense came. I say with my*
> *faith that they are forgiven from this point forward.*
> *I throw their sin into the sea of forgetfulness and*
> *mercy! Now, I command all unforgiveness and*
> *bitterness . . . Be plucked up by the root. In Jesus'*
> *Name, leave me. Leave my heart and life now! I*
> *command it in Jesus' Name and believe that it is*
> *done! Thank you Lord, for setting me free, and*

I'm quite sure...this is your 491st time!

delivering me from torment, trouble and all spiritual
defilement!
In Jesus' Name, Amen!

(I advise you to formally and prayerfully forgive every single person whom the Holy Spirit reveals to your heart. Let God heal you emotionally and set you totally free!)

I believe with you for the peace of God to now rule in your heart! I know that you have probably suffered at the hands of thoughtless and sometimes evil spirited people. **Life is hard. But aren't you glad that GOD IS GOOD!**

Chapter 8

"I HATE IT WHEN THAT HAPPENS!"

or

How do you deal with the disappointments of life?

Life is hard! Disappointments come. Things do not always work out as we hope. Perhaps your girl friend dumped you. Perhaps your husband left you.

Maybe you've lost a large amount of money on a business deal. Or maybe you were "taken" by a scam artist. Disappointment. It's tough to handle sometime. How do you do it?

I discovered an intriguing success story in the Bible a few years ago. It is the story of Barnabas, a man who faced disappointment in life, but overcame it!

The story begins in the upper room where one hundred and twenty believers were waiting for the arrival of the Holy Spirit. During their ten days of prayer and waiting, the Apostle Peter managed to carve out some Bible study time for himself. He discovered in the Psalms that a replacement for Judas the traitor, was to be found and appointed to the office of Apostle.

Peter shared this news with the others and mentioned that the new apostle should be someone who had followed Jesus throughout His entire ministry, from the baptism of John the Baptist up until His resurrection of which he must also have been an eyewitness. Two men were found who fulfilled these conditions. One was a man named Mathias. The other was Joseph Barsabas.

Mathias and Joseph are mentioned in the twenty third verse of Acts chapter one, where some Greek texts record Josephs' name as "Joses Barsabas." Interestingly, in *Acts 4:36* we read about "Joses Barnabas," and there some texts read "Joseph Barnabas." So it seems that the names "Joseph" and "Joses," as well as "Barnabas" and "Barsabas" are all interchangeable and therefore refer to the same man. So this man in the first chapter of Acts, nominated for Apostle, is Barnabas, a man mentioned several times in the history of the church during its early years. His is quite a success story.

Acts 1:23 states that Barnabas and Mathias were "appointed" to be considered for the apostolic position replacing Judas. This word, "appointed" literally means "to stand." So Mathias and Barnabas were "stood" before the congregation. They were selected as the only two possibilities, singled out publicly, and stood before the entire church.

I can see them right now in my mind's eye, standing in front of the room with Peter. A choice must be made. One of them is going to be the new leader!

For one of them, today is a great day of promotion! Yes, one of them will be officially APPOINTED to the office of Apostle!

Peter prayed this prayer:

"Thou, Lord, which knowest the hearts of all men, shew whether of these two thou hast chosen, that he may take part of this ministry and apostleship from which Judas by transgression fell, that he might go to his own place."

Now imagine how this sounded. May I paraphrase Peters' prayer? "Lord, you show us which one of these two men you have chosen for promotion. He must be very special, Lord! The ministry of an apostle is very important. It is an office of great power and authority. The RIGHT person must be chosen, Lord! And you must do the choosing, God, for you know their hearts! That's right, Lord. You know whether their hearts are right, or not right! You know if they are pure, or impure!"

"Lord, you know whether or not they are clean, sanctified, and holy. And you know if perhaps some dark, ugly, unclean, and scandalous motive lurks within the heart of one of these men.

You know all of the thoughts and intents of their hearts, God! You know which one of them deserves to be an apostle, and if one does not quite make the grade. Show us YOUR CHOICE, God! You choose the ONE YOU WANT! Amen."

At this time, (as was the custom of the day, having not yet received the Holy Spirit and knowing no better way to do it), they cast forth their lots. In other words, they drew straws. In a sense, they picked a name out of a hat, trusting God to guide their hands. Verse 26 states . . .

". . . the lot fell upon Mathias; and he was numbered
with the eleven apostles."

I can imagine that the room exploding with excitement, loud talking, and a round of applause for the newly appointed apostle. "Way to go there Mat!" "Congratulations boy!" "You have arrived!" "How does it feel, Mathias? Great, huh?" "Everyone come and shake Mathias' hand. Yeah, that's right, hug his neck!" "Come,

Mathias. Sit here with the other apostles." "You have a reserved seat now Mathias, right up front with James, John, Peter, and the rest of the leaders!" "From now on, we will refer to you as the Apostle, Mathias!" "Wow, what a blessing for Mathias!"

Yes, Mathias was APPOINTED! But where did that leave Barnabas? Well . . . DIS-APPOINTED!

"Okay Barnabas, you may return to your seat." "Better luck next time!" "You know Barnabas. It was the will of God." "Mat was God's choice." "What can we say?" "God knows the hearts you know!" "It was close, Barnabas" "You almost made it." "God knows the hearts." "Yes, Barnabas, God knows the hearts!" "You're all right aren't you Barnabas?"

Barnabas, slowly, with his head down, returned to his seat.

What do you suppose Barnabas was thinking? I'm not sure, but I know what he might have been thinking. He might have been thinking the same thing you or I might have been thinking, if we had been publicly disappointed like this.

"That unfeeling, uncaring, insensitive Peter! Does he not understand how he has made me feel?"

"Did he have to mention that 'God knowing the hearts thing?' Peter has humiliated me in front of the whole church! I am so embarrassed. I feel like crawling into a hole and dying!"

"Maybe, there is something wrong in my heart. I know, deep down that God has called me to be a leader, but maybe I have committed some terrible sin that disqualifies me. Am I even saved?"

"That stinking Mathias! Look at him. He's gloating! He's prideful. Why, he can't be God's choice. This is all wrong. Everybody knows I've paid a greater price than Mathias. Everybody knows I used to spend more time with Jesus than he ever did. Look at him. He thinks he is better than me! He has always been against me."

"That Peter, he was always against me too. I'll show him. I'll show all of them. I'm God's real choice. I'll go across town and start a new church. I'll call it 'Rival Bible Church.' It will be as big as theirs is."

I'm sure that Barnabas was tempted to think a lot of these things. But what did he do? The next mention of Barnabas is found in *Acts 4:36* where he is doing something that reveals a lot about his character.

The church was involved in a powerful outpouring of the Holy Spirit. Thousands were being born again. Miracles were happening.

The church was meeting daily, including many Greek speaking Jews who had stayed on in Jerusalem for an extended period of time, experiencing the move of the Spirit and receiving Christian teaching.

It was necessary to feed everyone. Therefore, free will offerings were being received. Some of the local believers there in Jerusalem, were giving very sacrificially. They were selling extra possessions and bringing the money and laying it at the Apostle's feet, which was their usual mode of giving. Look, here comes Barnabas.

Is Barnabas still around? Sure, he is! And, like many others, he has sold some land. He is bringing the money into the worship service. At the appropriate time, he makes his way to the front of the crowd and lays his offering down at the feet of the Apostles; Peter, James, John . . . and Mathias!

I think perhaps Barnabas has learned how to handle disappointment, don't you? He is not only still in the church. He is still submitted to the authority of the leaders! He still gives! He still worships! HE IS STILL FAITHFUL!

I mentioned that the story of Barnabas is a great success story! The Bible says that the apostles nick named Barnabas "son of consolation." They called him "Barnabas the encourager!" Somehow he had learned the art of encouragement and had gotten the victory over discouragement. I'm sure he had learned to be sensitive to people who had suffered disappointment!

May I also say that I think I know another reason why the Apostles nick named Barnabas "the encourager." Christians and church members like Barnabas, are some of the greatest encouragements a pastor can receive. So many allow disappointment to destroy their faith and their faithfulness. The "faithful" of the church really keep the leaders going! What an encouragement they are!

I mentioned that Barnabas is a great success story! Disappointment became appointment in his life because he learned how to guarantee the goodness of God.

In Acts chapter 9, Barnabas recommended a new convert by the name of Saul to the Apostles. They did not trust Saul at first because he had been a chief Jewish persecutor of Christians. Barnabas discerned that Saul was genuine in his faith and stood up for him. His act of kindness encouraged Saul who became Paul, the greatest Apostle of the early church.

When the Syrian city of Antioch received the gospel and many of its citizens were converted, the leaders at Jerusalem sent Barnabas to encourage the fledgling church. Barnabas had proven himself to the Apostles and was the prime choice for such a mission. Through Barnabas' ministry in Antioch many people were added to the Lord!

Later, Barnabas recruited Paul to come help him in Antioch. He always was one to include and promote others. And when a drought was prophesied for Jerusalem, the gentile Christians gave an offering for the poor saints there. Whom do you think they intrusted the cash to? Barnabas and Paul, who delivered the funds in person. Barnabas was always trustworthy!

In *Acts 12*, we read that Barnabas was a man who fulfilled his ministry assignments. Faithful Barnabas, what an encouragement!

And then in *Acts 13*, the day of promotion came in Barnabas' life! The Holy Spirit led the elders of the church to send Barnabas and Paul on a special apostolic missionary journey into gentile lands to advance the gospel and the kingdom of God! THIS WAS THE DAY THAT BARNABAS BECAME AN APOSTLE! *Acts 14:14* declares plainly that Barnabas became an apostle, the highest ministry office known to the church!

Barnabas made it! His humble character, sweet spirit, and FAITHFUL LIFESTYLE, caused him to be a winner.

DISAPPOINTMENT became APPOINTMENT because he discovered God's guarantee of goodness for his life!

GOD'S GOODNESS IS GUARANTEED WHEN YOU . . .

> ➤ **REMAIN FAITHFUL!**

REMAIN FAITHFUL to God and His Son, Jesus Christ!
REMAIN FAITHFUL to the scriptures and the character of Christ.
REMAIN FAITHFUL to the Holy Spirit's guidance in your life.
REMAIN FAITHFUL to your church, your pastor, and spiritual leaders.
REMAIN FAITHFUL to your dream, the vision that God gave you.
REMAIN FAITHFUL to your family, friends, and ministry partners.
REMAIN FAITHFUL to serve in your various areas of responsibility.
REMAIN FAITHFUL to fulfill your assignments.
REMAIN FAITHFUL to do the best job you can do.
REMAIN FAITHFUL to be an encourager of others, battling discouragement wherever it is found.

/

Chapter 9

"ET TU BRUTÉ"

or

How do you handle betrayal?

All of the subjects with which I have dealt in this book are close to my heart. I have great compassion for the sick and a great desire for them to receive physical healing from God. I desperately want to see people get their eyes off of their problems and focused upon the Saviour and His solutions.

I feel like I have fought failure in hand to hand combat throughout my adult life. Being a male, in a success driven society (and a church world) I have had to come to grips with failure, the fear of failure, success, and what true success is.

I know about life getting too heavy, too much and too hot to handle! I've had to learn how to forgive!

Many disappointments have come my way! I'm dealing with real issues here. These pages have been written straight out of my heart.

Twice, I have broken down emotionally as I worked on the manuscript. (I'm not usually a crier). Every subject we have taken up is serious and vastly important. I don't know though, if there is a subject more needful, or a hurt more real, or a hardship more powerful, than the one I address now.

Betrayal!

87

What could hurt worse than the betrayal of a trusted friend? What can crush the human heart more completely than a deserting spouse? What has the ability to scar the mind and emotions of a person more deeply than a mother throwing that person away as an infant?

Betrayal comes in many shapes, sizes, and styles. I could never address all of them. Most of us have been betrayed in some manner. Perhaps it happened within our family, or among our friends. It also occurs frequently at work, and I am sad to say, almost as often within the Church. Many are the shipwrecks of faith, caused by the selfish and sinful actions of so called "brothers and sisters" in the Lord!

What makes betrayal so devastating is that it can only be committed by those close to us. Betrayal is only possible among those who have obtained some sort of relationship, connection, information, or advantage with one another. Benedict Arnold's treason was noteworthy because he was an American. He was a traitor, not a spy. What made his act so despicable was that he was "trusted."

Betrayal is the breaking of trust!

Most of us have had the experience as a child, of revealing some greatly guarded secret to a friend or sibling. We trusted them totally to respect and guard it with their life, only to find that they immediately did the opposite. They told somebody, or they laughed at us, or they stole the precious find away from us. We learned one more lesson in the school of hard knocks. We learned early that trust is extremely risky!

THE RISK OF TRUST IS BETRAYAL.

God took the risk when He created Adam.

God took another risk when He saved Noah.

Moses took the risk when he traveled with Korah.

Samson took the risk when he loved Delilah.

Uriah took the risk when he married Bathsheba.

God took the risk again when He made covenant with Israel.

God took the risk again when Jesus invited Judas to follow Him.

God took the risk again when He made covenant with the Church.

GOD TOOK THE RISK AGAIN WHEN HE INVITED YOU TO FOLLOW JESUS!

I don't suppose anyone has been betrayed more than God. Has your family forsaken you? So did God's. Has your wife committed adultery? So has God's.[1] Was betrayal an element in your divorce? It was the reason behind God's divorce as well.[2]

God became a man, Jesus Christ. Jesus lived our life, experienced our problems, and felt our hurts. He was tempted in all ways in which we are.[3] He knows what we are going through. He genuinely senses our pain.[3] He was betrayed too. Jesus can help us. God can help us overcome betrayal![4]

The Psalmist prophesied that Jesus the Messiah would be betrayed by His own friend.

> *"Yea, mine own familiar friend, in whom I trusted, which did eat of my bread, hath lifted up his heel against me."*
>
> *Psalm 41:9*

Jesus knows all about betrayal! Judas was His disciple, employee, associate, assistant, treasurer, confidante, and friend. Judas had prospered greatly from the relationship. Jesus had fed him, clothed him, and trained him for more than three years. Jesus had made huge investments into the life of Judas. Jesus loved Judas. He LOVED him!

Then Judas, on the same night in which he ate at Jesus' table, shared Jesus' bread and dipped sauce from Jesus' bowl, took inside privileged information, and sold it to Jesus' murderers. Afterwards, when he did the deed, executed the betrayal, and ruthlessly broke Jesus' trust, he did it with the very token of trust, love, and friendship. He did it with a kiss. A cold, unfeeling, uncaring kiss!

Let me guess. That's how they did it to you too.

I thought so. That's how they did it to me!

"Jesus, help us."

Jesus will help us. Let's read a passage from the word of God and discover how!

> *"Wherefore seeing we also are compassed about with so great a cloud of witnesses, let us lay aside every weight, and the sin, which doth so easily beset us, and let us run with patience the race that is set before us, looking unto Jesus the author and finisher of our faith; who for the joy that was set before him endured the cross, despising the shame, and is set down at the right hand of the throne of God. For consider him that endured such contradiction of sinners against himself, lest ye be wearied and faint in your minds."*
>
> *Hebrews 12:1-3*

God encourages us to look unto Jesus, the beginner and the perfecter of our faith, if we are to successfully run the race of life. God will get you to the finish line, but you must keep your eyes on the goal. We must keep our eyes on Jesus!

Betrayal is an attempt by your spiritual adversary, Satan, to convince you to quit the race. Betrayal is so emotionally destructive that it has the power to do just that. For when people grow weary and faint spiritually, according to verse three, it happens in their MINDS. If Satan is to defeat you Christian, he knows he must defeat you in your mind, your thinking, your will, your emotions. Betrayal is an all out attack upon your mind!

Jesus is at the finish line cheering us on, beckoning unto us to finish and win our race! He ran the race before us. He suffered betrayal and endured His cross! He can help us finish and win!

We must run the race LIKE HE RAN IT! We must FIND OUT HOW HE WON HIS RACE!

Verse three says that He *"endured such contradiction of sinners against himself."* In other words He was patient and enduring even while sinful men did terrible things to Him. This includes every deed of mockery, injustice, and painful torment, but it also includes the betrayal of Judas. This one evil deed was what instigated and brought about all of the sufferings of Jesus on the cross!

HOW was Jesus able to handle His betrayal?
"Jesus . . . who for the joy that was set before him endured the cross . . . "

Hebrews 12:2

There was a "joy" which was "set before" Jesus enabling Him to endure His suffering! If it was "set before" Him, then He was LOOKING AT IT! He was FOCUSED ON IT! His mind was SET UPON IT!

This "JOY" evidently was well worth suffering for. It was well worth dying for. What was it? What was Jesus' joy?

The greatest joy of Jesus was the purpose for which He lived and died. His greatest joy, His vision, His dream, His goal, was the SALVATION OF THE WORLD FROM ITS SIN!

John the Baptist said, *"Behold the lamb of God which taketh away the sin of the world."*[5] This is what Jesus was all about! Judas' betrayal could not compete with Jesus' dream. In fact, Judas' betrayal assisted Jesus in realizing His dream. It actually VAULTED JESUS INTO THE FULFILLMENT OF HIS DREAM!

Your betrayals can assist you in reaching your dream as well! Suffering and betrayal play their parts in pressing you toward the fulfillment of your God given destiny. That is, IF YOU FOCUS ON JESUS!

It is not what happens to you in life that makes you or breaks you, but rather how you respond to those things! The lies they tell on you cannot hurt you! They may injure someone else's opinion of you, but they cannot change you unless you let them. Ignore them. KEEP YOUR EYES ON JESUS!

Your divorce cannot stop you! Their rejection cannot cripple you! Anyone who would betray you is not capable of helping you to realize your divine potential. You don't need any relationship which is detrimental to your dream!

Their betrayal cannot hinder you or even slow you down. Rather, it will help to speed you toward your destiny, for their betrayal is a reminder for you to GET YOUR EYES ON JESUS!

FOCUS ON JESUS!

FOCUS ON THE JESUS THINGS IN YOUR LIFE!

FOCUS ON HIS ASSIGNMENT IN YOUR LIFE!

FOCUS ON THE DREAM AND VISION THAT HE PLACED IN YOUR HEART!
FOCUS ON THE JOY HE HAS SET BEFORE YOU!

FOCUS ON HIS GOALS IN YOUR LIFE!

SET YOUR EYES ON THE FINISH LINE AND DON'T BE DISTRACTED!

WINNERS FOCUS ON THE PRIZE, NOT THE PAIN!

GOD'S GOODNESS IS GUARANTEED WHEN YOU . . .

A JESUS FOCUS is how you were saved and began your race toward God's destiny in the first place. Just like the Israelites fixed a steady gaze upon the brazen serpent on the pole and were healed of their snake bites, YOU FIXED a STEADY GAZE OF FAITH UPON JESUS ON THE CROSS and you were healed of your sin. By continuing to focus in faith upon Jesus YOU ARE CONTINUALLY HEALED OF SATAN'S SNAKE BITES IN YOUR LIFE.

KEEP YOUR JESUS FOCUS!

Betrayal is tough. Life is hard. But always remember . . .

GOD IS GOOD!

Chapter 10

"I CAN'T FIND A JOB!"

or

What do you do when no one will hire you?

I began working my first job in 1968. I was fifteen years old and made fifty cents an hour. My boss's name was F.M. Babb. He was a pharmacist and hired me to be a clerk in his drug store. I received stock shipments, filled the shelves with magazines, greeting cards, toiletries and medication, and ran the cash register. Mr. Babb taught me a great lesson.

"There is always something to do!"

He would say that all the time. He was fond of repeating it. I heard it . . . and heard it . . . and heard it. He really drilled it into me. "There is always something to do."

Mr. Babb did not pay me fifty cents an hour to stand around. He expected me to be busy. To be perfectly honest though, I did stand around some. There were times when I just couldn't find anything to do! I didn't enjoy doing nothing. It was boring and an hour would seem like an eternity, especially if Mr. Babb was the druggist on duty. If Mr. Babb was there, I had to act like I was busy! It was miserable to act like I was busy while doing nothing!

I would never go tell Mr. Babb that I had run out of work though. I thought he might give me something hard to do. Or worse yet, he might make me clean shelves.

Cleaning shelves was boring and tedious work. I hated cleaning shelves, so I never asked Mr. Babb for suggestions. If he wanted me to do something, he had to tell me.

Every once in a while Mr. Babb would notice I was having trouble staying busy. So he would come out from behind the counter, walk up to where I was acting busy, and say, "David, there is always something to do!" "Yes sir, Mr. Babb," I would reply. "I was just doing such and such." Or I would say, "I was just about to do this and that," or "I've just finished so and so." Mr. Babb would say, "I have something else I need you to do."

He would find something too. Usually it was cleaning shelves. I never wanted to clean shelves and I didn't want to get caught, but it did help pass the time to be doing something. In fact, working was a lot easier than trying to look like I was working when I really wasn't.

When Mr. Babb found things for me to do, it reinforced what he had taught me. I figured out that there was always something to do. If I began to doubt the truth of that statement, I was quickly reminded that Mr. Babb could always find me something to do. There was no end to the jobs that could be found in that little, small town, drug store. There was always something to do. Usually, there were a lot of shelves that needed cleaning!

So, you don't have a job! Well, there is plenty to be found. I know there is! Do you know how I know? Mr. Babb told me . . .

"THERE IS ALWAYS SOMETHING TO DO!"

We live in a big world. If there was always something to do in that little drug store, I know that there is something you can do in this great big world! And if you're having trouble finding it, God is a great big God and I know that He can help you!

The entire Bible teaches the work ethic. The first man Adam, was given a job before he was given a wife or a family. No one is created to stand around. Some people try to act busy for God, but He is even smarter than Mr. Babb. He knows what's going on! He has some real work for you to do. He loves for all of us to stay busy. In fact God has some very hard hitting words for anyone who refuses to work!

". . . if any would not work, neither should he eat."

2 Thessalonians 3:10

According to God, there is only one class of people that ought to feel obligated to work, produce, and stay busy. Everyone else can take an eternal break, go on a permanent vacation, and maybe just stand around a lot and look busy! But if you are one of THOSE WHO EAT, you really need to be working! Does that seem hard? Well, that's because LIFE IS HARD!

"I'm not against working. I just can't get anyone to hire me!" you say. Really? I believe that there is always something to do! Not just because Mr. Babb said it, but because God said it! Listen!

"But my God shall supply all your need, according to his riches in glory by Christ Jesus."

Philippians 4:19

We often quote this promise as we teach God's people about His willingness to prosper their lives and meet all of their financial needs. I have meditated on it, quoted it, and confessed it by faith practically every single day for almost twenty years. I live by this promise. I love this promise! But did you know that this verse is also talking about you getting a job?

Oh yes, it does promise that God will supply your needs. But what about a guy or gal that is experiencing difficulty landing a job? This verse covers that too!

The word translated "need" can also be translated "EMPLOYMENT!"

". . . my God shall supply all your EMPLOYMENT"

I like that. God will give you a job! You say that no one will hire you? GOD WILL!

I challenge you to believe God. Ask Him to supply your employment, believe you receive it, and you shall have it. (See *Mark 11:24*).

Now, I challenge you to do something else. GO TO WORK!

That's right. Go out and go to work!

"Well I don't know where to work yet," you say. Let me help you. Go to work finding your job. Why don't you spend eight hours a day looking for something to do?

If you're going to have a job, you're going to have to have something the old timers used to call "gumption." Let me tell you about gumption.

I know of a man who needed a job. He married at a young age and had a family to support by the time he was sixteen or seventeen years old. He applied for a construction job, but he was under age and they told him that they couldn't hire him. He really needed a job so he decided that he would go to work anyway. Do you know what he did? Now this is "gumption!"

He put on his work clothes and packed himself a lunch. Then he went down to the construction site and went to work. They told him again. "We can't legally hire you, son. You're under age!" The young man said, "Well I'll just work for free. I've come to work and I'm going to work!"

He worked several days for free but did such a fine job, they finally bent the rules for him and put him on the payroll. They were embarrassed for him to be working without pay and besides that, he was working so hard that they didn't want to do without him. He basically made them hire him! The guy had "gumption."

There is always something to do!

Back when gasoline was fifty cents a gallon, the news media was predicting that it would eventually be raised to a dollar. I was horrified. I asked my father-in-law one day, "What in the world are we going to do if gas goes to a dollar a gallon?" He said, "We'll just have to make more money!" He had "gumption." His "gumption" changed my thinking. Sometimes, you have to make more money.

Sometimes you will have to go to work. If you will take this attitude, God will hire you at something!

Why don't you find something you are good at, and go to work for yourself? Sell something. Make something. Fix something. Create something. Write something. Teach something. Announce something. Advertise something. Clean something. Clean some shelves! But do something! If you aren't good at anything, learn something. Go back to school. Become an apprentice. Read a book. Equip yourself in some way for success!

Invest eight hours a day learning, searching, thinking, moving, giving, serving, or ministering to someone. There is always something to do. Do you want to show God that you are not lazy? Go to the church where you attend and ask the pastor for something to do. Don't call him on the phone and say, "If you ever need anything just let me know." He's too busy and overworked to remember that. Go down there. And don't get bent out of shape if he has someone else put you to work instead of giving you personal attention. Do you want a job, or just someone to pet on you? Do it with all your heart. Now you will be working for God, and God will be obligated to pay you!

Do you think I sound like I have no compassion? If so, then you're wrong. I do have compassion. I know what it's like to have a wife and a child, and not be able to find work. I also know what it's like to work twelve hours a day, yet the money you earn doesn't cover your budget. I've got compassion. I've been there. On the other hand, I need to tell you something that my stepfather taught me.

"It's a cold cruel world out there!"

"I wish I'd never started reading this chapter," you say? Well, I'm sorry. Someone has to wake you up. At the age of eighteen and fresh out of high school I took a job as a deckhand on a Mississippi River towboat. I worked for Mid-America Transportation Company, a coal hauling operation, out of St. Louis, Missouri. This was one of those jobs where you work, eat, and sleep on the boat for thirty to forty days at a time. I started this outdoor manual labor job in the winter of 1971. I didn't know how to dress for a job like that and I didn't take enough warm clothes. I thought I was going to freeze to death. It wasn't just the weather that was cold, I found out that people are too. I realized that, "it's a cold cruel world out there!"

My stepfather had been right. I found out that nobody cares whether or not I succeed, except God and myself. That may sound negative, but it's the truth. If you want to work, if you want to succeed, if you want to accomplish anything, you need to develop your relationship with God. Begin to trust Him and begin to do something about your situation because faith without "works" is dead.[1] However if you will believe and act, God will help you!

GOD IS GOOD! He will hire you! He wants you to work!

GOD'S GOODNESS IS GUARANTEED WHEN YOU . . .

➤ PUT YOURSELF TO WORK

Believe me. There is always something to do. Put yourself to work doing something. I like what Pastor John Osteen says:

"Let us do something, lest we do nothing!"

I've seen some people turn down jobs when they had no job, just because they thought the pay was too low. Hello! Any pay is better than no pay. I know. They think that they are worth more than what the job offered. Let me tell you something. If they were worth very much, the world would be knocking their door down trying to hire them! There is a shortage of hard working people these days. Hard workers are at a premium.

Has anyone ever taught you how to keep a job? May I suggest some things while we are dealing with this subject?

1.   **FIND OUT WHY YOUR EMPLOYER HIRED YOU.**
You might be shocked to know how many people spend a lot of their work day doing things their boss doesn't even want them doing. Then when their employment is terminated, they don't understand why! Find out what your employer desires from you and then do it.

2.   **ARRIVE A LITTLE EARLY AND STAY A LITTLE LATE.**
Average workers don't ever get ahead. You have to do something notable to be noticed. Give your employer a full days work. As a Christian, go the second mile. Adopt the motto, "And then some!"

3.   **AT THE BOTTOM OF YOUR JOB DESCRIPTION ADD THIS CLAUSE; "AND ANYTHING ELSE THEY ASK ME TO DO."**

I never cease to be amazed at the people who after being fired, or quitting a job, will try to justify their departure with, "Well I'm sorry, but they wanted me to do things which I didn't hire in to do!"

4. **REMEMBER AT ALL TIMES FOR WHOM YOU ARE WORKING.**

You don't work for the other employees, so why try to please them? You don't work for the union. You are not working for yourself, so you can't just do what you please. You are hired to make your employer successful. Pursue that with all your might!

God is good! He will supply you with employment. If you will PUT YOURSELF TO WORK, He will bless you! He blesses what you put your hand unto![2] Because of His GOODNESS, **He GUARANTEES blessing when you OBEY His Word by FAITH!**

Chapter 11

"HURRY UP GOD.
I DON'T HAVE ALL DAY!

or
How do you handle waiting on God's timing?

One day I learned something from Lacey. I call it the "Lacey Lesson." Lacey is the youngest of our three daughters, the baby. I'm very proud of all of my girls. They're wonderful girls. They love and serve Jesus!

That's a good testimony for preachers' kids. Many preachers' kids hate God, hate church, and hate their parents. The life of a minister and his family is sometimes extremely hard!

We were leaving the house to go somewhere . . . again. I was trying my best to get everyone headed toward the car. The door was standing wide open and Lacey, a toddler at the time, was on the front porch.

She turned and saw me standing in the entry way. Then she stepped back inside. She looked up at me and with her little hands on her hips, said sternly, "Huwwy!" ("Huwwy!" being interpreted means "hurry!")

Now, what makes this so sad, and informative, is that this is the first word Lacey ever said. Not dada. Not mama. Oh no!

"Huwwy" was my little girl's first clearly spoken word. Well, almost "clearly spoken." I learned something that day. We say "hurry!" a lot at my house. We are always in a hurry. Lacey had possibly heard the word "hurry" more times than any other word. Isn't that sad?

One day just a couple of years ago as we were rushing home in our car, Lacey, who was then nine years old, told me, "Dad, the world is not spinning as fast as you think it is!" Hmmmmm! I don't guess I've slowed down much.

I'm still in a hurry. I still say "hurry" a lot around my house. I know that I also try to hurry God. It's very frustrating to me that He doesn't seem to be in as big of a hurry as I am. My wife isn't. My kids aren't. And God isn't either. I feel like it's a great conspiracy to frustrate me! Doesn't anyone understand how much we have to do? Well, if you turned to this chapter first, then you're sort of like me aren't you? In a hurry! So tell me, why are you "doing time?"

IS IT A MATE you're waiting for? You hate weddings for the simple reason, YOU are not in them! If you are asked to be the bride's maid or the best man, you hate that worse. Too close for comfort, right?

IS IT A FINANCIAL BREAKTHROUGH that is taking some time? You're a tither, a giver, a pledge payer, and a prayer, and you are confessing your faith, but you're still in debt, in need, in lack, and in trouble if God doesn't move quickly! Yeah, I know quite a few people sitting in that waiting room!

IS IT BUSINESS OR CAREER SUCCESS that is eluding you? You work hard, stay sharp, make good suggestions, and continually go the second mile, but the boss hasn't noticed you yet? He doesn't even know your name?

IS IT A RELEASE INTO YOUR MINISTRY CALLING that seems to be withheld from you? You know you're called. You're ready. You're anointed. You have new, fresh ideas. You have received illumination on the scriptures right out of Heaven. You are a natural born leader and people like you! But . . . the door of ministry just hasn't opened!

IS IT AN ANSWER TO PRAYER you are waiting for? You've claimed the promise. You believe you have received according to *Mark 11:24*.

You are confessing it by faith every day. But the manifestation of your answer hasn't come! Oh, how well I know your situation!

In all honesty, any of the aforementioned situations could be being held up by your own lack of Biblical knowledge or action. There are times when we think we are waiting on God, but actually GOD IS WAITING ON US!

Now, this is another lengthy subject which I won't get into here. But I do advise you to learn anything and everything about the issue you are dealing with. Then with all of your heart and might, pursue your goal in God through proper action and faith. I believe that God will give you victory in every area of your life!

Sometimes however, we really are waiting on God.

I've noticed something about God.

GOD SELDOM GETS IN A HURRY.

He waited four thousand years after promising a redeemer to Eve, before Jesus was born to a virgin in Bethlehem. After Jesus was born, He waited until He was thirty years old before He began His ministry.

God waited until Moses was eighty, before sending him back to Egypt to liberate the Israelites.

God waited forty years for the unbelieving Israelites to die off so that He could help the younger believing generation possess the land of promise.

Were these years of waiting, wasted? Isn't that how we feel? We often think that "time waited, is time wasted."

TIME WAITED IS NOT TIME WASTED!

God spent thousands of years, showing the world His perfection and power as opposed to its wickedness and weakness. Then, just at the right time, He sent a Saviour.

Jesus was a man. Yes, He was God, but God in the flesh of a man. As a man He had to grow in wisdom and in stature. He wasn't ready to save the world in one day. He spent thirty years in preparation.

He didn't make all of those parables up as He went, okay? As He reached the age where society could begin to listen to Him, He began to minister and share God's love with them.

His years of preparation were not wasted!

God waited forty years for Moses to learn the ways of Egypt and to discover the futility of those ways when Moses found himself murdering an Egyptian. Then God waited forty more years as Moses learned the ways of God and how to lead God's people by leading a flock of sheep on the backside of a desert. God was not wasting time, He was investing time in Moses.

God had no choice but to wait for the young Jewish generation of faith. There was no way that unbelieving and disobedient people could have ever established a great nation in Canaan. God's kingdom is built through faith and obedience, and God waited for these holy character traits to emerge in His chosen people. God was not wasting His time.

GOD IS GOOD! He doesn't desire to frustrate us, but rather to FURNISH us with the equipment we need to succeed, then clean us, mature us, complete us, perfect us, and polish us, until we have developed a high gloss FINISH. He desires us to be *"vessels unto honor,"*[1] not just clay pots but fine china in the household of faith! Believe me, your time spent in waiting is not wasted because . . .

GOD IS WORKING!

Do you desire God in His goodness to take charge of your life? Do you want God to work out the details for you? Have you made enough "messes" and suffered with enough of your own plans and decisions that you are willing for God now to do it HIS WAY? Then I suggest that you WAIT ON GOD!

His timing is accurate! His wisdom is infinite! His plan is perfect!

GOD'S GOODNESS IS GUARANTEED WHEN WE . . .

> ## ➤ BELIEVE THAT GOD IS AT WORK

Here are some promises God has made to you right out of the "Good News!"

". . .be ye steadfast, unmoveable, always abounding in the work of the Lord, forasmuch as ye know that YOUR LABOR IS NOT IN VAIN in the Lord."

1 Corinthians 15:58

"And let us not be weary in well doing: for IN DUE SEASON WE SHALL REAP, IF WE FAINT NOT. As we have therefore opportunity, let us do good unto all men . . ."

Galatians 6:9-10

"Trust in the Lord, and do good, so SHALT THOU DWELL IN THE LAND, and verily THOU SHALT BE FED. Delight thyself also in the Lord; and HE SHALL GIVE THEE THE DESIRES OF THINE HEART. Commit thy way unto the Lord; trust also in him; and HE SHALL BRING IT TO PASS. And HE SHALL BRING FORTH THY RIGHTEOUSNESS AS THE LIGHT, and the judgment as the noonday. Rest in the Lord, and wait patiently for him: fret not thyself because of him who prospereth in his way, because of the man who bringeth wicked devices to

pass. Cease from anger, and forsake wrath: fret not thyself in any wise to do evil. For evil doers shall be cut off, BUT THOSE THAT WAIT UPON THE LORD, THEY SHALL INHERIT THE EARTH. For yet a LITTLE WHILE, and the wicked shall not be..."

Psalm 37:3-10

God puts "little whiles" in our life. How long is a "little while?" Well, it's a little while! God tells us though how to endure the "little whiles." You read it in the passage above.

"WAIT UPON THE LORD!"

Our problem is that we do not understand what God means when He tells us to wait upon Him. We assume He means to sit still, to sit idle, to do nothing until He gets ready to do something.

This is actually the opposite of what God wants.

In the passage above there are two different Hebrew words translated "wait." The first one means "to TWIST, to WHIRL, or to DANCE." The second one means "to BIND TOGETHER BY TWISTING."

The Jews along with many Christians today, worshiped God with dance. They would dance and whirl and turn their bodies as a form of praise and worship in the glorification of God.

God does not want us to sit idly by and wait on some mysterious something to happen. HE DESIRES US TO WORSHIP HIM! HE WANTS US TO REJOICE IN HIM! HE WANTS OUR

111

LIVES TO BE LIVES OF CELEBRATION, LIVES OF DANCING AND WHIRLING AROUND HIM AS OUR GOD AND KING!

A rope is "bound together by twisting." God desires you to BECOME BOUND TOGETHER WITH HIM BY TWISTING. In other words, He wants you to twist yourself around Him, His principles, His promises, and His ways, to the point where you are. . . ALL WRAPPED UP IN GOD!

GET ALL WRAPPED UP IN GOD!
BELIEVE THAT GOD IS WORKING!

(This is how you can guarantee His goodness in your life).

Ask yourself a question, "How can I get wrapped up in God, relative to my situation? What does God desire out of me WHILE I WAIT ON HIS BLESSING IN MY LIFE? What is God working into me, what is God doing in me, during this season in my life?"

Here are some practical hints: If you are WAITING ON A MATE, why not consider this? What kind of mate would be the kind of mate you desire, and want? I mean, you're picky, right? You know, you could probably be married already, except you are a little bit picky about what kind of mate you're going to get! Well, what if they are picky too?

What kind of mate would they deserve? Are you that kind of person? How can you become that kind of person? Why don't you get wrapped up in God until He makes you what you need to be? As the old saying goes, "You need to dance with the one that brung ya!" He knew how to get you where you are and He knows how to get you where you're going!

If you are WAITING ON A FINANCIAL BREAK-THROUGH, you need to get wrapped up in God, seek first His kingdom, practice biblical stewardship (tithing, giving, and budgeting), and you need to study God's plan for abundance in your life, in the Bible. Study finances. Find the changes that need to be made in your financial life. Obviously, you are going to have to change something! If you continue to do what you are doing, you will probably continually get the same results!

If you are WAITING ON BUSINESS OR CAREER SUCCESS, get wrapped up in God. He is number one! He is your partner! He wants you to succeed, so don't "religiously" assume He isn't interested in your success. He simply wants it correctly prioritized in your life. Be open to His guidance and character development. He will bring promotion into your life![2]

If you are WAITING ON A RELEASE INTO YOUR MINISTRY, first realize you are already released into ministry of some sort! It may not be your ultimate calling. It may not yet be a total fulfillment of your ministry dream and vision.

Guess what, neither is mine after twenty years! But you can minister right now! Get all wrapped up in God, the things of God, the people of God, and the work of God. God blesses doers! Don't have "pewy religion" just sitting on a church pew.

Rise up and begin to do! Get involved in the blessing of others. Be a blessing and you will be blessed!

If you are WAITING ON AN ANSWER TO PRAYER, get all wrapped up in the Word of God. Get all wrapped up in the promises. Then get all wrapped up in the conditions which the Bible spells out that must be met to receive your answer. (Almost all of God's promises are conditional). Then get all wrapped up praising God that His Word is true, and that your answer is on its way! Confess your faith, walk your faith, act your faith, and live your faith.

Decide once and for all that you will not take no for an answer. If you are waiting on God, you are waiting, not hearing no! If God said it in His Word, He will do it! As my friend, Hardy Brundage, often says, "If God's got it, you can have it!"

REMEMBER, TO WAIT IS NOT A WASTE OF TIME.

WHILE WE ARE WAITING . . .

GOD IS WORKING!

CONCLUSION

I would like to share a final word with you. It is a deep revelation of truth. (It must be deep because many sincere believers, ministers and even theologians seem to have trouble understanding it or at least communicating it). Here it is:

GOD IS GOOD!

Sound simple? It is. And yet isn't it profound? God is good! He is not evil. God is your friend! He is not your enemy. God will help you! He will never hurt you. God is on your side! He isn't against you.

Why not begin to trust Him again? Begin to believe and obey His word again. You can lean on His everlasting arms. He will never let you down!

God is good! Believe it and His goodness will begin to fill your life!

GOD IS GOOD!   BELIEVE!

REFERENCES

Chapter 1
[1] Galatians 3:13-14
[2] 1 Peter 2:24
[3] Matthew 27:46, Ephesians 1:6
[4] Mark 9:23
[5] Hebrews 11:6
[6] Romans 10:9-10
[7] Acts 2:47, Hebrews 10:24-25
[8] Luke 18:1 I Thessalonians 5:17
[9] 2 Timothy 2:15, Romans 10:17
[10] Matthew 28:19, Acts 2:38
[11] Acts 2:4, Acts 19:6
[12] Hebrews 10:24, Proverbs 18:24, 1 John 1:7
[13] Acts 2:42, 2:46, 3:1, 5:42

Chapter 2
[1] Genesis 1:28
[2] Genesis 1:26
[3] Job 2:7 Luke 13:16, Acts 10:38
[4] Matthew 8:16-17
[5] James 5:14-15
[6] Mark 16:17-18
[7] Mark 11:24
[8] Mark 11:23
[9] Mark 5:36
[10] Hebrews 13:8

Chapter 3
[1] Hebrews 11:6   [2] 1 John 5:4

Chapter 4
[1] John 8:32
[2] 1 John 5:4

Chapter 5
[1] Luke 17:32

Chapter 6
[1] Genesis 2:24
[2] Genesis 2:18
[3] Proverbs 18:22
[4] Deuteronomy 6:5-7
[5] Psalm 127:3
[6] Psalm 127:4-5

Chapter 7
[1] Mark 9:23
[2] Luke 23:34
[3] 1 Corinthians 13:5-7

Chapter 9
[1] Jeremiah 3:8
[2] Isaiah 50:1
[3] Hebrews 4:15
[4] Hebrews 4:16
[5] John 1:29

Chapter 10
[1] James 2:26
[2] Deuteronomy 28:12

Chapter 11
[1] 2 Timothy 2:21
[2] Psalm 75:6

GOOD NEWS EVANGELISM!

David & Connie Brown are on the go. . .taking the good news of a good God to hurting people on the mission fields of the world. Miracles, healings, signs and wonders accompany the Good News of Jesus Christ!

An eight year old
girl shares her tes-
timony of healing
from stomach can-
cer in the "Fiesta
de Milagros"
(party of miracles)
Campaign in
Comayagua,
Honduras.

An automobile
accident left this
woman in great
pain and on
crutches for five
years. She was
healed in a local
church campaign
in Saltillo, Mexico.

Connie celebrates with two ladies, both healed of arthritis in Tegucigalpa, Honduras.

This little "señorita" was healed of total deafness! Her miracle occured in the Saltillo Mexico Campaign in which **1000** people testified to being healed and **900** people prayed to receive Jesus as Lord and Saviour.

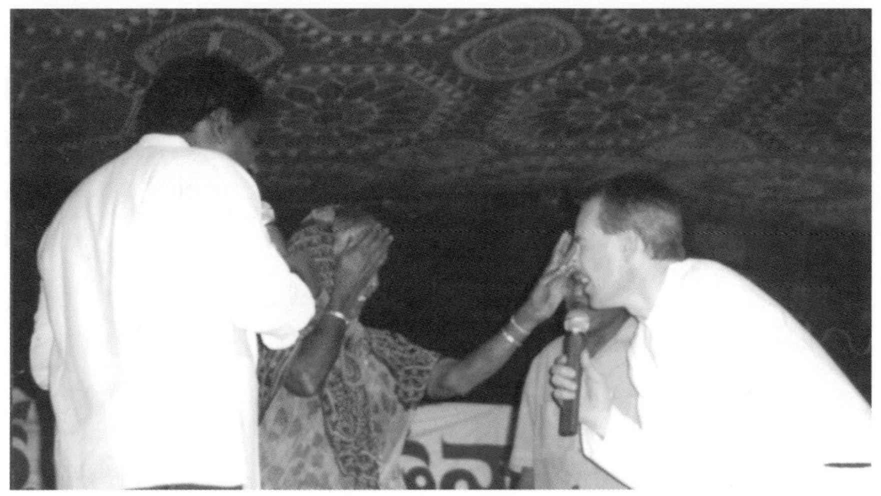

This woman, sight restored to her totally blind left eye, proves her healing by finding David's nose. . .Miryalguda, India.

This eight year old boy
was healed of total deafness
 in his right ear
...Miryalguda, India.

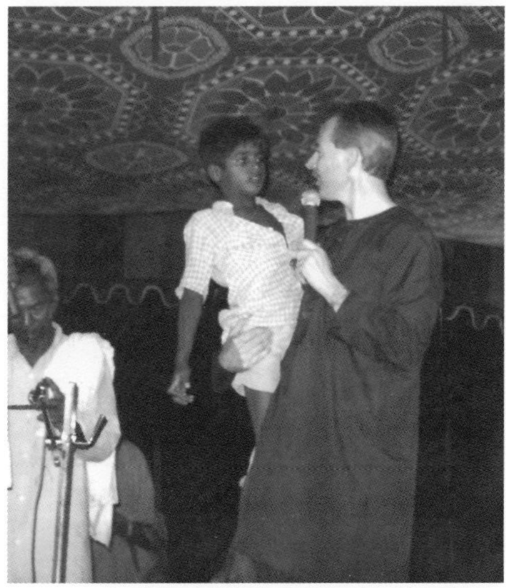

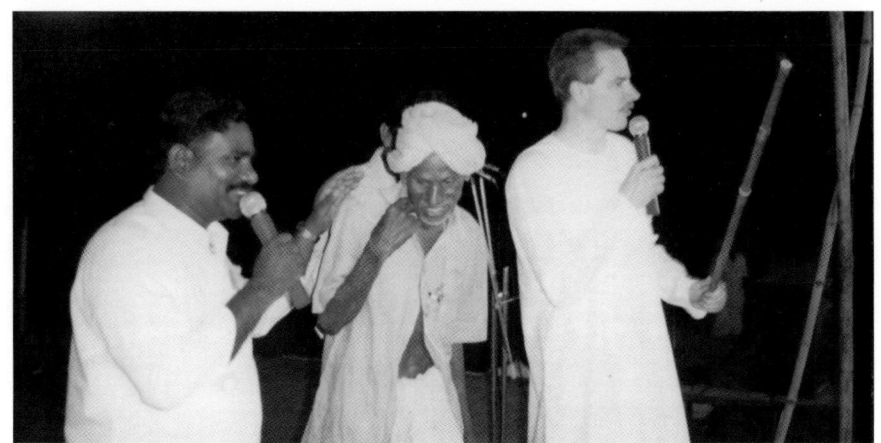

Above: This man doesn't need his walking stick anymore. He was totally healed of lameness. . . Miryalguda, India.

Below: Pastor David encouraged the people of Miryalguda, India to put their trust in Jesus Christ for forgiveness and miracles!

Below: Visiting and teaching a Banjara tribe in Southern India

Miryalguda, India Crusade in 1995

In 1974, David Brown received a vision from God. He saw himself proclaiming "Jesus Christ is the Saviour of the world" to masses of dark sinned people in open air meetings. Convinced that God's goodness and miracle power are the biblical keys to mass evangelism, David Brown is presently focused on evangelizing every major city of Honduras, by the year 2000. Faith partners are needed to help fulfill this vision.

Become a partner with me
in Good News Ministry!

to help me TELL THE WORLD that "God is Good!"

Your financial support of this ministry will enable us to continue and expand these vital ministry projects:

SALVATION/HEALING CAMPAIGNS
➤ We conduct campaigns in several nations of the world including India, Mexico, and Honduras with doors

also opening in Pakistan. Our present focus is upon the nation of Honduras with a goal of conducting campaigns in every medium and large city in the nation, by the year 2000.

MINISTRY TRAINING

➤ In addition to training ministers through our local church ministry in Amarillo, Texas, we are equipping ministers, leaders and church members for leadership, evangelism and church growth on the foreign mission fields of the world.

LITERATURE

➤ We are providing Bibles and Christian books equipping and edifying the body of Christ.

MEDIA

➤ Presently ministering through local radio from Victory Church in Amarillo, we plan to expand into television ministry in the very near future.

To contact David Brown for ministry engagements, you may write to:

David Brown
P. O. Box 32121
Amarillo, TX 79120
Telephone: (806)359-9463
Fax: (806)359-9498

Dear David,

❑ I want to become a monthly ministry partner and help you share "Good News" with a lost world! Enclosed is my first monthly gift of
$__________

❑ I am not able to become a monthly partner at this time, but am enclosing my one-time gift of $__________

Name __________________________________

Address _______________________________

City ____________________ State________Zip________

Phone _________________________________

Clip & Mail Today!

Mail to:
David Brown Ministries
P.O. Box 32121
Amarillo, TX 79120

"Following the Flow of God"

God's supernatural power can flow through you. People can be saved, healed, strengthened, and set free, as the Holy Spirit ministers through you.

Pastor David Brown teaches three simple keys to recognizing and releasing the Holy Spirit, into the lives of the people who need a touch from God. You can be used of God. The gifts of the Holy Spirit can flow through you. Lives will be dramatically changed, by the power of Jesus Christ, as you learn to "Follow the Flow of God."

This book and additional copies of **"Life is Hard but God is Good"** are available from your local bookstore or by contacting:

David Brown Ministries
P. O. Box 32121
Amarillo, TX 79120
Telephone (806) 359-9463
Fax (806) 359-9498

For Reorders Contact:
Walk on the Water Faith Church
PO Box 1124
Osage Beach, Mo. 65065-1124 USA
573-348-9777 / Web: www.faithman.org